GRADES 6-8

BRAIN-COMPATIBLE
ACTIVITIES

DAVID A. SOUSA

Skyhorse Publishing

Visit our website at www.skyhorsepublishing.com.

10 9 8 7 6 5 4 3 2 1

Library of Congress Cataloging-in-Publication Data is available on file.

Cover design by Lisa Riley

Print ISBN: 978-1-63450-372-3
Ebook ISBN: 978-1-5107-0114-4

Printed in China

GRADES **6-8**

BRAIN-COMPATIBLE
ACTIVITIES

TABLE OF CONTENTS

Connections to Standards **4**

Introduction **6**

Put It Into Practice **7**

CHAPTER 1
Language Arts **9**
Activities and reproducibles

CHAPTER 2
Mathematics **28**
Activities and reproducibles

CHAPTER 3
Social Studies **46**
Activities and reproducibles

CHAPTER 4
Science **65**
Activities and reproducibles

CHAPTER 5
Physical Education and the Arts **82**
Activities and reproducibles

Answer Key **95**

References **96**

Connections to Standards

This chart shows the national academic standards that are covered in each chapter.

LANGUAGE ARTS	Standards are covered on pages
Read a wide range of literature from many periods in many genres to build an understanding of the many dimensions (e.g., philosophical, ethical, aesthetic) of human experience.	16
Apply knowledge of language structure, language conventions (e.g., spelling and punctuation), media techniques, figurative language, and genre to create, critique, and discuss print and nonprint texts.	22
Develop an understanding of and respect for diversity in language use, patterns, and dialects across cultures, ethnic groups, geographic regions, and social roles.	10
Use spoken, written, and visual language to accomplish a purpose (e.g., for learning, enjoyment, persuasion, and the exchange of information).	25

MATHEMATICS	Standards are covered on pages
Numbers and Operations—Understand numbers, ways of representing numbers, relationships among numbers, and number systems.	29
Algebra—Use mathematical models to represent and understand quantitative relationships.	42
Measurement—Understand measurable attributes of objects and the units, systems, and processes of measurement.	34
Data Analysis and Probability—Formulate questions that can be addressed with data, and collect, organize, and display relevant data to answer them.	38

SOCIAL STUDIES	Standards are covered on pages
Understand the ways human beings view themselves in and over time.	47
Understand individual development and identity.	54
Understand relationships among science, technology, and society.	60
Understand the ideals, principles, and practices of citizenship in a democratic republic.	63

SCIENCE	Standards are covered on pages
Physical Science—Understand properties and changes of properties in matter.	78
Life Science—Understand structure and function in living systems.	70, 74
Earth and Space Science—Understand structure of the earth system.	66

Introduction

Brain-compatible activities are often louder and contain more movement than traditional lessons. Research has shown that purposeful talking and movement encourage retention of new learning. While this may seem out of your comfort zone at first, good classroom management and a willingness to try new things is all that is needed to implement these activities in any classroom. Once you and your students become accustomed to brain-compatible strategies, you will find it difficult to go back to more traditional teaching methods. Students (and teachers!) enjoy lessons that actively involve their brains, and the brains that are actively involved are the brains that learn.

It has been estimated that teachers make over 1600 decisions per day. As professional educators, it is our job to be familiar with current research to make sure those decisions count for our students. This book is filled with activities that are supported by brain research. These activities will help increase learning because they are structured to maximize the brain's learning potential.

How to Use this Book

The activities in this book are designed using a brain-compatible lesson plan format. There are nine components of the plan, but not all nine are necessary for every lesson. Those components that are most relevant to the learning objective should be emphasized.

- Anticipatory set
- Learning objective
- Purpose
- Input
- Modeling
- Check for understanding
- Guided practice
- Closure
- Independent practice

Each of the components is described in detail in the book titled *How the Brain Learns, Third Edition* (2006). Refer to it for more brain-compatible research and other teaching strategies.

When using the activities in this book, read through the activity first. Then begin the preparations for the lesson. Make sure to follow the lesson plan format to ensure maximum learning potential. However, be flexible enough to meet the needs of all learners in your class. A positive classroom climate is essential for retention.

Put It into Practice

How the brain learns has been of particular interest to teachers for centuries. Now, in the twenty-first century, there is new hope that our understanding of this remarkable process called teaching and learning will improve dramatically. A major source of that understanding is coming from the sophisticated medical instruments that allow scientists to peer inside the living—and learning—brain.

As we examine the clues that this research yields about learning, we recognize its importance to the teaching profession. Every day teachers enter their classrooms with lesson plans, experience, and the hope that what they are about to present will be understood, remembered, and useful to their students. The extent that this hope is realized depends largely on the knowledge base teachers use in designing those plans and, perhaps more important, on the strategies and techniques they select for instruction. Teachers try to change the human brain every day. The more they know about how it learns, the more successful they will be.

Some of the recent research discoveries about the brain can and should affect teaching and learning. For example, this research has:

- reaffirmed that the human brain continually reorganizes itself on the basis of input. This process, called neuroplasticity, continues throughout our life but is exceptionally rapid in the early years. Thus, the experiences the young brain has in the home and at school help shape the neural circuits that will determine how and what that brain learns in school and later.

- revealed more about how the brain acquires spoken language.

- developed scientifically based computer programs that dramatically help young children with reading problems.

- shown how emotions affect learning, memory, and recall.

- suggested that movement and exercise improve mood, increase brain mass, and enhance cognitive processing.

- tracked the growth and development of the teenage brain to better understanding the unpredictability of adolescent behavior.

A much fuller explanation of these discoveries and their implications for school and the classroom can be found in my book, *How the Brain Learns, Third Edition* (2006), published by Corwin Press. This book is designed as a practical classroom resource to accompany that text. The activities in this book translate the research and strategies for brain-compatible teaching and learning into practical, successful classroom activities. They focus on the brain as the organ of thinking and learning, and take the approach that the more teachers know about how the brain learns, the more instructional options they have at hand. Increasing teachers' options during the dynamic process of instruction also increases the likelihood that successful learning will occur.

Some general guidelines provide the framework for these activities:

- Learning engages the entire person (cognitive, affective, and psychomotor domains).

- The human brain seeks patterns in its search for meaning.

- Emotions affect all aspects of learning, retention, and recall.

- Past experience always affects new learning.

- The brain's working memory has limited capacity and processing time.

- Lecture usually results in the lowest degree of retention.

- Rehearsal is essential for retention.

The activities in this book also are backed by research-based rationale for using particular instructional strategies, including cooperative learning groups, differentiated instruction, discussion, movement, manipulatives, metaphors, movement, visualization, and so on, all of which can increase motivation and retention of learned concepts. Those who are familiar with constructivism will recognize many similarities in the ideas presented here. The research is yielding more evidence that knowledge is not only transmitted from the teacher to the learners but is transformed in the learner's mind as a result of cultural and social influences.

The classroom is a laboratory where teaching and learning processes meet and interact. This laboratory is not static but constantly changing as intensive research produces new discoveries about how the brain learns and retains information. The more information educators have, the more they can adjust their understanding and instructional strategies to ensure students are using their brains to the fullest capacity. As we discover more about how the brain learns, we can devise strategies that can make the teaching-learning process more efficient, effective, and enjoyable.

CHAPTER 1
Language Arts

The human brain is not hardwired for reading. Our brains can master spoken language quickly. However, because the act of reading is not a survival skill, the brain requires explicit training in reading. Learning to read requires three neural systems and the development of skills that work together to help the brain decode abstract symbols into meaningful language. The visual processing system sees the printed word, the auditory processing system sounds out the word, and the frontal lobe integrates the information to produce meaning. It is a bidirectional and parallel process that requires phonemes to be processed at the same time. Reading is testament to the brain's remarkable ability to sift through input and establish meaningful patterns and systems.

Reading is one of the most difficult skills for the brain to master, and it is even more difficult when students must make the jump from learning to read to reading to learn. It is crucial, therefore, that the activities chosen for use in language arts programs capture students' attention and promote retention.

As the brain is decoding the meaning of sounds and symbols, it is creating semantic and syntactic networks that aid in communication. Verbal and written communication involves syntax and semantics to create meaning. The syntactic network uses the rules of language, or grammar. The semantic network combines the components of language and the mind's search for meaning. The brain holds two separate stores for semantics, one for verbally based information and another for image-based information. Using concrete images to teach abstract concepts will greatly increase retention. The brain builds on speaking skills to develop and refine all language abilities—speaking, reading, writing, and grammar.

> The scientific research suggests that reading instruction include a balance between the development of phonemic awareness and the use of enriched texts to help learners with syntax and semantics.

Idiom Interviews

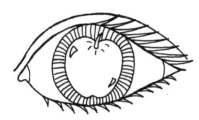

Standard

Develop an understanding of and respect for diversity in language use, patterns, and dialects across cultures, ethnic groups, geographic regions, and social roles.

Objective

Students will demonstrate an understanding of idioms in the English language.

Anticipatory Set

◄ Make a transparency of the **Common Idioms reproducible (page 13)**. Ask students to listen as you read the phrases and evaluate if the phrase is positive or negative. Tell students they should stand if the phrase is a positive one. They should sit if the phrase is a negative one. They should put their hands on their heads if they don't know. Read the phrases from the Common Idioms page. Watch students to see if they are participating, but do not make judgments about their knowledge.

Common Idioms Page 13

Purpose

Tell students they are going to learn about idioms and their meanings. They will use creative thinking to interpret idioms.

Input

Talk to students about idioms. Remind them of the idioms you used in the Anticipatory Set part of this lesson. Ask them to reflect on any other idioms they hear used at home, school, or other places. Define the word *idioms* and discuss why idioms are unique parts of a language.

Tell students they are going to interview adults on campus to generate a list of idioms common to our region of the country. Then they are going to think about those idioms literally and figuratively.

PART 1—The Interviews

Modeling

Because idioms are figures of speech, they are not formally taught. Users of a language grow to understand idioms by hearing them used. Different areas of the country may have idioms that have meaning only in that region. Students will interview adults on campus to generate a list of common idioms in your area.

> "Providing familiar examples will help students apply meaning to the new learning later in the lesson."

Give each student a copy of the **Idiom Interview reproducible (page 14)**. Put a transparency of it on the overhead projector. Think aloud as you demonstrate how to complete the reproducible. At the top of the reproducible, show students how to complete the definition and examples of idioms. Encourage students to use words that make sense to them.

Show students where they will record the information they gather during the interview (at the bottom of the reproducible). Encourage students to prepare questions before the interview. Have students role play conducting an interview with a partner. They should alternate roles so both students get to practice asking the questions.

Idiom Interview Page 14

Check for Understanding

Use a quick assessment technique to check for understanding. Ask a student to explain the task in his or her own words. Review the directions if necessary.

Guided Practice

Send students to conduct their interviews. Be visible on campus for accountability and to help as needed.

It is important to talk about your expectations of students' behavior when they are out of the classroom. Remind students to never interrupt a class. There are many adults on campus who are happy to assist as long as the interview does not take very long and they are given some prior warning. Consider people such as the resource specialist, office staff, custodial staff, and cafeteria personnel. Discuss appropriate manners and speaking when interviewing someone. With careful student preparation and monitoring, brief, on-campus interviews are an effective teaching strategy.

Send students in groups of two or three to conduct interviews. Allow about five to ten minutes for students to conduct the interview. Remind students to return to the classroom before the time is up. If you monitor students by leaving the classroom with them or enlisting the help of adult chaperones (parent volunteers, aides, other teachers), you can avoid "strays." Consider telephone calls if movement around campus is not an option or if there is a limited pool of interview subjects.

Closure

As students return, have them list their idioms on sticky notes. Write *Idioms* on a piece of chart paper. Invite students to place the sticky notes on the chart in the front of the room. Read the idioms aloud to the class.

PART 2—The Visual

Modeling

Crazy Idioms Page 15

◄ Make a transparency of the **Crazy Idioms reproducible (page 15)**. Model how to complete the activity. Think aloud about an idiom you find humorous (For example, *raining cats and dogs*). Tell students you researched the origin of the idiom and found that it might be based on an old English custom of placing hay on the roofs of houses. Animals such as dogs and cats would sleep there and subsequently fall off the roof in a downpour of rain. Demonstrate where to write the idiom and its possible origin. Show students how to cite the source from which they obtained the information.

Then show students where to draw an image of the idiom. For example, if it is raining cats and dogs, you might draw a picture of a house with cats and dogs tumbling down from the sky. Show students they can be creative and have fun with the drawings!

Check for Understanding

Use a quick assessment technique to check for understanding. Try asking students to show a thumbs up if they understand and a thumbs down if they need another explanation.

Guided Practice

Give each student a copy of the Crazy Idioms reproducible. Remind them of the chart the class made containing the list of idioms. Prompt students to choose one idiom and write it on the reproducible.

Allow students access to computers and art supplies to complete the activity. Play background music (no lyrics). Circulate and assist as needed. Monitor Web searches closely as some sites may not be suitable for students.

Closure

Allow students to share their work and display them in the room. Consider creating a Crazy Idioms book. Collect all the reproducibles and compile them into a book. Share the book with other classes.

> **Background music (no lyrics) with 60 beats per minute can enhance creativity and productivity.**

Common Idioms

"apple of my eye"

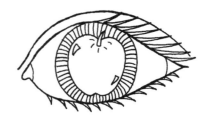

"backseat driver"

"chip on his shoulder"

"got up on the wrong side of bed"

"can play by ear"

"not playing with a full deck"

"tied the knot"

"was saved by the bell"

"is under the weather"

"minds his Ps and Qs"

"is as sharp as a tack"

Idiom Interview

Directions: Complete each of the following sentences.

An idiom is _____

_____

An idiom can be peculiar because _____

_____

Examples of idioms are _____

_____

_____

The person I interviewed was _____

Idioms he or she uses regularly are

_____

_____

Idioms he or she has heard before but does not use are

_____

_____

_____

Crazy Idioms

Directions: Write the idiom. Write the origin of the idiom.
Create a visual image of the idiom.

Idiom:

Origin:

Source:

Uninvited to Tea

Standard

Read a wide range of literature from many periods in many genres to build an understanding of the many dimensions (e.g., philosophical, ethical, aesthetic) of human experience.

Objective

Students will read, research, and dramatize characters from a novel.

Anticipatory Set

This activity works best after your class has read a novel. While many reading strategies are effective, literature circles work exceptionally well when more than one book is read at a given time. If you are unfamiliar with this strategy, take advantage of the many resources available to guide you. Literature circles are powerful, brain-compatible options for middle school students.

Pretend you are the White Rabbit from *Alice's Adventures in Wonderland* by Lewis Carroll. Race into class checking your pocket watch like the White Rabbit and speaking as if you are in a rush. *We're late. We're late. Oh, dear me! Whatever shall we do? There's a party to attend and none of you are ready. Oh, we must hurry to prepare. What? You did not know about the tea party? Why it's the Mad Hatter's Tea Party, and you are all invited. Or, well, uninvited, but we have to get ready.*

> Applying knowledge increases the level of thinking required.

Purpose

Tell students they are going to become characters from a novel and attend a tea party.

Input

Remind students of the novel(s) they have been reading. Ask students to name the novel(s) and provide a brief summary of the plot. Guide a discussion about characters and their importance in a novel. Give a short lesson on characterization using examples from the novel(s) students have been reading.

Tell students each of them will become a character from the novel they have read. The characters will gather for a tea party in the classroom on the designated day to talk about themselves. You will provide students with some reproducibles to help them prepare their role and instruct them on the appropriate behavior for a tea party.

Modeling

Give each student a copy of the **Character Analysis reproducible (page 19)**. Demonstrate how to complete the reproducible using one of the characters from a novel. Think aloud about how you answer the questions, and show students how to refer back to the novel for reminders and evidence.

The concept map will help students organize their ideas about how to portray the character at the tea party. Show them how to complete the **In Character reproducible (page 20)**. Remind students that other people in ▶ the class may not be familiar with the novel or its characters and to plan their actions and conversations accordingly.

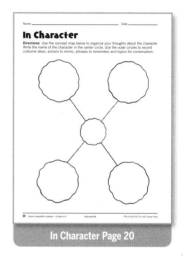

In Character Page 20

Check for Understanding

Use a quick assessment technique to check for understanding. If students understand what to do, have them hold up one finger. If they do not understand, have them hold up two fingers. Review instructions as necessary.

Guided Practice

Write the names of characters from the novel(s) on index cards. Assign the characters by asking students to draw a card. You may allow students to switch gender specific cards if desired.

Remind students they will need to understand how the character interacts with others and any traits that make that character unique. On a prearranged date, the class will have a tea party. Involve parents by requesting each student bring a traditional tea party contribution (tea cakes, tea, finger sandwiches, etc.) Encourage students to dress as the character for the party. Students should be prepared to act like the character during the party, using phrases and behaviors unique to the character. Students will use the Character Analysis reproducible and the In Character reproducible to help them prepare.

Allow time for students to complete the reproducibles. Assist as needed.

Closure

On the assigned day, prepare the classroom for a tea party. Arrange the party goods and food in a way that will facilitate conversation. When the party begins, have students get into costume and character. Hold students accountable for remaining in character and encourage conversation around the table. Make sure you talk to each student, so each can portray his or her character.

Independent Practice

Reflections Page 21

◄ Have students complete the **Reflections reproducible (page 21)** for homework or as a class assignment the following day.

Name _____ Date _____

Character Analysis

Directions: Answer the questions below. You may refer back to the novel.

_____
(book title)

1. Assigned character: _____

2. Description of character: _____

_____

_____

3. Character's role in the plot: _____

_____

_____

4. How does the character interact with others? _____

_____

_____

5. What phrases or actions are repeated by the character? _____

_____

_____

_____

In Character

Directions: Use the concept map below to organize your thoughts about the character. Write the name of the character in the center circle. Use the outer circles to record costume ideas, actions to mimic, phrases to remember, and topics for conversation.

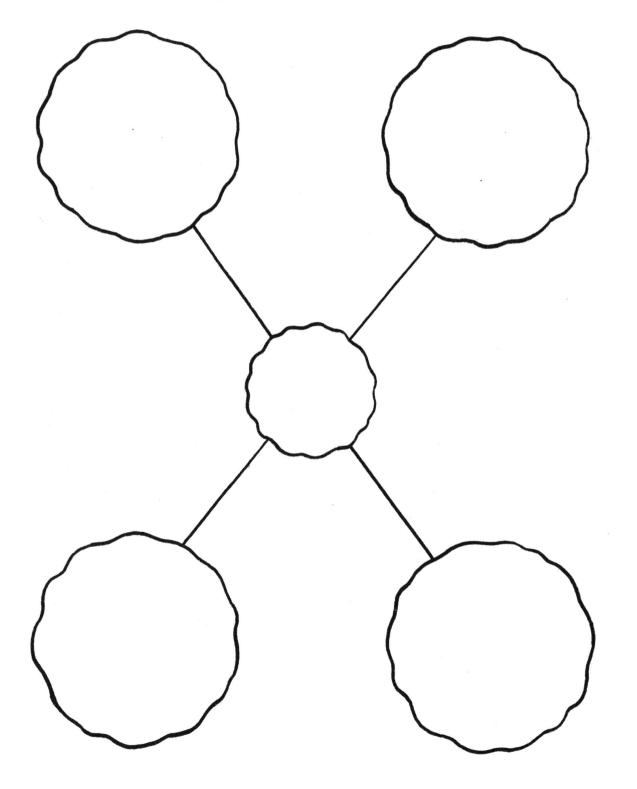

Reflections

Directions: Reflect on the character tea party.

_____
(book title)

My favorite part of the book was _____

because _____

_____

The character I researched was _____ . I am like my character

when _____

_____

I am different from my character because _____

_____

I think this book is _____ (interesting/not interesting) because _____

_____

I would give myself a _____ (grade) on my reading/research because

_____

I would give myself a _____ (grade) on my character portrayal because

_____

I did my best work when I _____

I could have done a better job at _____

_____   _____
(Signature)   (Date)

Sinking Sub

Standard
Apply knowledge of language structure, language conventions (e.g., spelling and punctuation), media techniques, figurative language, and genre to create, critique, and discuss print and nonprint texts.

Objective
Students will demonstrate knowledge and application of the prefix "sub".

Anticipatory Set
Challenge students to a game of "Simon Says." Play in the usual manner, except make sure everything you tell them to touch is under another object. For example, tell students: *Touch the legs under the desk. Touch the floor under your feet. Touch the sleeve under your arm.*

Purpose
Tell students they are going to learn about the prefix *sub-*.

Input
Give a brief lesson on prefixes. Remind students that prefixes are added to the beginning of a word. Since most prefixes have their own meanings, their addition can change the meaning of a root word. By learning the meaning of a prefix, one can often figure out the definition of unfamiliar words.

Ask students to write down as many words as they can that begin with the prefix *sub-*. Allow about one minute for students to write. Invite volunteers to read their lists aloud. Record the words on the board or chart paper where everyone can see.

Review the list aloud, correctly pronouncing every word. Ask students to consider the words and what the prefix *sub-* might mean. Allow adequate wait time. Encourage students to think about the game you played at the beginning of the lesson and the list of words in front of them. Prompt students to write their answers on a small white board and show you the answer. Celebrate the correct answer and reinforce that *sub-* means "under."

Give each student a copy of the **Sinking Sub reproducible (page 24)**, and demonstrate how to complete it. Show them how to draw a picture in each box to visually represent the meaning of the word. Think aloud as

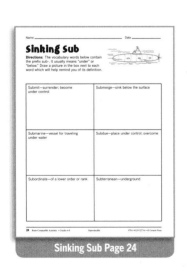

Sinking Sub Page 24

you say the word, say the definition, and think about what to draw. Give students several minutes to process the words. When time is up, have students walk quickly around the room, touch five objects which are under another object, and return to their seats. Direct students to share their pictures with a person sitting near them.

Modeling

Model how to write a fictional story as a group using the words from the Sinking Sub reproducible. Ask three students to join you at the front of the room. Form a circle and sit on the floor or at tables arranged in a circle. Write the first sentence of the story on a piece of paper. Then pass the paper to the person on your left. He or she will write one sentence and pass the paper to the left. Continue this way until all students in the class understand the procedure. This writing technique is not complicated but can be difficult to explain. Modeling helps ensure every student understands the process prior to the start of the activity.

Check for Understanding

Use a quick assessment technique to check for understanding. Ask students to raise their left hand if they understand or raise their right hand if they do not understand.

Guided Practice

Divide students into groups of four. Prompt students to write a story about any topic, but remind them it must contain all of the words on the Sinking Sub reproducible. The group must keep writing until the time is up. Therefore, they can continue to pass the paper around the circle even after everyone has contributed. Set a timer for 10 minutes for this activity. Monitor teams closely to ensure each student is contributing.

Closure

Invite a representative from each group to read their story to the class. Display the stories on the bulletin board next to a list of the vocabulary words as part of your print-rich environment.

Independent Practice

Have students highlight words that start with *sub-* in a newspaper or magazine for homework. Ask them to bring the papers back to class, and add them to the bulletin board display.

> **Movement provides fuel to the brain.**

Sinking Sub

Directions: The vocabulary words below contain the prefix *sub-*. It usually means "under" or "below." Draw a picture in the box next to each word which will help remind you of its definition.

Submit—surrender; become under control	Submerge—sink below the surface
Submarine—vessel for traveling under water	Subdue—place under control; overcome
Subordinate—of a lower order or rank	Subterranean—underground

Hink Pink Think!

Standard

Use spoken, written, and visual language to accomplish a purpose (e.g., for learning, enjoyment, persuasion, and the exchange of information).

Objective

Students will expand their vocabulary usage and knowledge of synonyms.

Anticipatory Set

Take a crumpled piece of chart paper (or a stress ball) and toss the ball to a student. As you toss the ball, say a word, such as *big*. Tell the student who catches the ball to give a synonym for the word you said. That student then tosses the ball to another student and he or she gives a synonym. Keep the ball moving for one minute. List the synonyms on a piece of chart paper as they are called out.

Purpose

Tell students they are going to stretch vocabulary and critical thinking skills as they have some fun with synonyms and rhyming words.

Input

Show students the list of words you created during the game. Lead a discussion about synonyms and rhyming words. Make sure to mention the similarities and differences of synonyms and rhyming words. Synonyms are words that have a similar meaning. Rhyming words are words that have a similar sound. It might be helpful to write the words *synonym* and *rhyme* on the board and list the similarities and differences.

Tell students they are going to be creating and figuring out word puzzles called Hink Pinks. Hink Pinks are pairs of rhyming words that are synonyms to word clues.

Modeling

Give each student a copy of the **Hink Pink Think reproducible (page 27)**. Point out the examples at the top of the page and demonstrate how to decipher Hink Pinks. Think aloud about the clues and how to find the answer. Model how to determine the answer by searching for synonyms for each word of the clue until you find two that rhyme.

Hink Pink Think! Page 27

Ask students to complete the rest of the page with a partner. Suggest they take turns sharing answers until the entire page is finished. Praise or coach students and make sure everyone understands the answers. Allow five minutes to complete the task. At the end of the time limit, go over the answers by calling on students randomly. Move on to model the next part of the activity.

Give each student an index card. Model how to create a Hink Pink. On one side of the card write the clue. On the other side, write the answer. Think aloud as you generate the Hink Pink.

Check for Understanding

Use a quick assessment technique to check for understanding. Ask students to put thumbs up if they understand or thumbs down if they need more clarification. Repeat instructions as needed.

Guided Practice

Give students a few minutes to think and write an original Hink Pink on the index cards. The easiest way to write a Hink Pink is to think of the answer first and then write a clue to match. Assist as needed.

When students are ready, instruct them to mingle around the room. When you say *Think!*, students must turn to the person nearest them and simultaneously show the clue on their card. Ask students to guess the Hink Pink on their partner's card. When everyone has had a chance to guess, prompt students to wander around again. Repeat the process as many times as you'd like. Be sure to wander through the class making sure students are mixing with different partners.

Closure

Have students return to their seats and give a cheer to the Hink Pink Champs. Have students complete the bottom of the Hink Pink Think reproducible for closure as they sip pink lemonade.

> **Higher-level thinking can increase motivation and retention.**

Name _____ Date _____

Hink Pink Think!

Directions: Hink Pinks are pairs of rhyming words that are synonyms to given clues. Write the Hink Pink for each clue on the line beside it.

Examples:			
Noisy Cumulus	*Loud Cloud*	Strange Whiskers	*Weird Beard*
Scarlet Cot	*Red Bed*		

1. Enormous Feline _____ _____

2. Fat Hog _____ _____

3. Dark Bag _____ _____

4. Overactive Pampers _____ _____

5. Final Dynamite _____ _____

6. Icy Jewelry _____ _____

7. An Insect's Jeans _____ _____

8. Little Swimsuit _____ _____

9. Empty Seat _____ _____

10. Dirty Cat _____ _____

11. Yacht Election _____ _____

12. Distant Automobile _____ _____

Write the Hink Pink you created, as well as two others you learned today.

_____ _____ _____

CHAPTER 2

Mathematics

> ## You cannot recall information that your brain does not retain.

Mathematics is often the least favorite subject for both students and teachers. A common misconception about math is that facts and figures cannot be fun, so lecture is often the primary strategy used to impart this wisdom to the next generation. Lecture, however, has been proven the least effective method for long-term retention. It is no wonder students develop a disdain for math. It is hard to like something you struggle to retain.

The following activities are proof that mathematics objectives can be taught in brain-compatible ways and can actually be (dare we say it?) fun! Since math concepts on paper are abstract, one of the easiest ways to make them more brain-compatible is to use concrete strategies, such as movement and manipulatives.

A math journal is a great way to help students reflect on the concepts taught during math instruction. Taking time to reflect on new learning or applying new concepts to promote higher-order thinking can both enhance retention of material and be accomplished effectively in a journal.

Is it a Deal?

Standard

Numbers and Operations—Understand numbers, ways of representing numbers, relationships among numbers, and number systems.

Objective

Students will compute advertised sale prices to determine the most efficient use of a given monetary amount.

Anticipatory Set

Face the board and write, *Everyone who is seated and giving me full attention when I turn around gets an A on the next test.* Turn around and say, *Wonderful! You all get an A on the next test and here it is . . . an A on top of everyone's next test!* Place a wooden block with the letter A on a stack of papers.

Purpose

Tell students they are going to be analyzing some advertisements to determine the best way to spend a budgeted amount of money.

Input

Consumers are hit every day with advertisements promising the best deal. Truth-in-advertising laws prohibit outright lying in ads, but crafty marketers can stretch the truth. Shoppers must use caution to make sure the promised bargain is just that.

Advertisements try to lure consumers with special sale prices on merchandise. Often these incentives include a percentage off the regular price, free items when something else is purchased, and rebates. In the real world, most consumers have limited resources with which to purchase the items they need and

want. It is important, therefore, that they make those resources go as far as possible. Calculating the actual price of items regardless of the advertised sale is a necessary skill for a smart shopper.

Talk to students about advertising and budgeting. Try to relate the discussion to students' own lifestyle concerns. *If you have $20, can you buy the jeans you want? Which store has the best price on your favorite CD? If your allowance is $10, how long will you have to save to get the skateboard you want?* Guide the discussion around how companies use advertising to lure customers. Encourage students to think about how consumers can be tricked by advertising or use advertising to get the best deal.

Modeling

On an overhead projector, compose a fictional sale on shoes. Tell students you want to buy two pairs of shoes. They normally cost $30 each. One store is offering a buy-one-pair-and-get-a second-pair-for-half-off sale. Another store has a coupon for 20% off the entire purchase. Think aloud about which store will offer the best deal.

Ask students to help you determine which math skills will be useful in solving the problem. *What math skills will you need to compute the best deal?* Ask students to list those skills on small white board or piece of paper. Allow adequate wait time. Invite students to share their list with a partner. Encourage the partners to add any information that was missing. Call on random students to tell one skill and list it on chart paper or the overhead transparency. Skills should include multiplying fractions, calculating percentages, and computing money.

If students are not familiar with multiplying fractions, calculating percentages, and computing money, teach the skills before continuing the lesson. If students already know the concepts, review the required skills to activate prior knowledge. Demonstrate how to solve the problem using your example about the shoe sale. Think aloud as you solve the problem.

Check for Understanding

Provide another example on the overhead transparency. Give students an opportunity to solve the problem on their own and write down the answer on their small white board or paper. When students have completed the problem, ask them to place the white board or paper face

> **Applying knowledge in real-life scenarios creates meaning for students.**

up on the desk. Walk around the room and quickly scan the answers to see that everyone has gotten the correct answer. Review the skills as necessary.

Tell students they are going to use the same skills and procedures to complete the activity. Clarify the task as needed.

Guided Practice

Tell students they will have $100.00 to spend on clothing. They need to buy as much as they can with the budget they are given. Give students a copy of the **Super Saver Times reproducible (page 32)**. It contains all the advertised sale prices on the items students can purchase. Have students work in groups to review the advertisements and determine how to spend the $100 and get the best deals.

Encourage students to use the **Is it a Deal? reproducible (page 33)** to help guide them as they work the problems. While they may work with a group, each student must complete his or her own worksheet. It is acceptable for team members to have different selections. The primary use of teams in this scenario is to provide support for the mathematical skills necessary to work the problem. Play background music with 60 beats per minute (no lyrics). Circulate and assist as needed.

Closure

Have students answer the following questions in their math journals. *Why is it important for you as a consumer to know how to compute decimals and fractions? Why do you need to be wary when you read advertisements? What did you learn about the difficulties of staying within a budget?*

Independent Practice

Have students find an advertisement at home. Ask them to figure the price of sale items of ten items for homework.

Super Saver Times Page 32

Is It a Deal? Page 33

Super Saver Times

25 cents

A Daily Newspaper

Jeans–Buy two pairs for $24 each
& get a third pair **FREE**

Backpacks

$24 for Deluxe $15 for Regular

Shirts

40% OFF

the regular price
of $19.99

OLD SAVVY

Average Consumer & Thrift

Shirts – 20% OFF
regular price of $15

Jeans – $19 per pair

Shoes – Buy one pair at $50 &
get the 2nd pair 1/2 off

Extra 10% OFF on entire
purchase if you open a credit
card account with 18% interest

STRAPPED

Backpacks – 30% OFF
regular price of $30

Jeans – $65 & you get a
FREE

CD

of your favorite band

Shirts – Buy two at $12 each
and get one **FREE**

Shoes –$39.99 after mail-in
REBATE of $20

Backpacks – 2 for $30 or
1 for $20

Jeans – $29 per pair

Shirts – $16 each

Shoes – $40 per pair

Extra 20% OFF
Everything you stuff in your bag

Moody's

Is It a Deal?

Directions: Use the Super Saver Times to find the best deals on items you will need for school. You have $100 to spend. You must buy at least one of each of the following: jeans, shirts, backpacks, and shoes. The total quantity of each item is up to you. Compute the actual cost for the sale items to help you make wise choices. Be prepared to defend your decisions with facts. Show your work on the back of this page.

Actual Final Costs for Jeans:

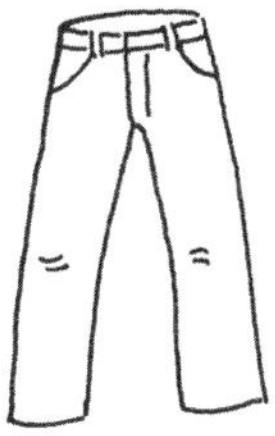

Old Savvy _____

A & T _____

Strapped _____

Moody's _____

Actual Final Cost for Shoes:

Old Savvy _____

A & T _____

Strapped _____

Moody's _____

Actual Final Cost for Shirts:

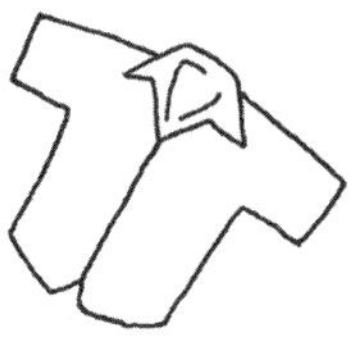

Old Savvy _____

A & T _____

Strapped _____

Moody's _____

Actual Final Cost for Backpacks:

Old Savvy _____

A & T _____

Strapped _____

Moody's _____

Your Sales Receipt

Store	Item	Quantity	Cost
		Total:	

Metric Measurement Relay

Standard

Measurement—Understand measurable attributes of objects and the units, systems, and processes of measurement.

Objective

Students will accurately measure length using metric units.

Anticipatory Set

Divide the class into groups of four students. Ask the groups to brainstorm a list of games or sports in which the winner is the one with the lowest score. Have one person from each group report on the list and record all the responses on the board.

Purpose

Tell students they are going to learn about measuring with metric units while playing a balloon relay game.

Input

Give a brief lecture about the metric system and its importance. Begin by comparing the metric system to the U.S. Customary System to activate prior knowledge. Emphasize the use of prefixes in the metric system and how they can help students calculate measurements. Give each student a copy of the **Metric Relay reproducible (page 36)**. Refer to the reproducible and use visual clues and examples when explaining the units of measure. For example, show a metric ruler. Mark a meter on the board. Mark a centimeter. Mark a millimeter.

Metric Relay Page 36

Modeling

Model how to play the balloon relay game. Give each team a meter stick and review how to use it. Give each person on the team a balloon of a different color. Show students how to play the game. Stand at the starting line. Blow up the balloon, but do not tie it. Let the balloon go, and see where it lands. Use the measuring stick to measure how far away the balloon landed. Make sure to use detailed measurements, and record them on the Metric Relay reproducible. The next person on the team will stand next to where the first balloon landed and repeat the procedure. The team measures the distance and continues until they reach the finish line. (Note: remind students not to put their mouths on another student's balloon.) The winning team is not necessarily the team who finishes first. Rather, it is the team with the lowest total measurements—the most direct path to the finish line.

Check for Understanding
Make sure teams understand the relay procedures and how to use the meter stick for measurement.

Guided Practice
Prepare a starting line and a finish line in a large clear space, such as the playground or a gymnasium. The course should be a straight line of about 10–15 meters from the starting line to the finish line.

Line up the teams at the starting line, and give the signal to start. The first person on each team will blow up the balloon and release it. The team measures from the starting line to where the first balloon landed. The team records the measurement on the Metric Relay reproducible. Then the second person on the team blows up his or her balloon and releases it. The team measures from where the first balloon landed to where the second balloon landed, records the measurement, and repeats the procedure until they reach the finish line.

Closure
Celebrate the winning team with a class cheer. Have students answer the following questions in their math journals. *Do you think the metric system is easier or harder than the system you are used to using? Why? Convert your team's total meters in the relay to centimeters and millimeters. Refer to your worksheet for help.*

Independent Practice
Have students complete the **Metric Math reproducible (page 37)** for homework.

> **Journal writing is a great closure for the learning episode and a way to refocus students after a stimulating activity.**

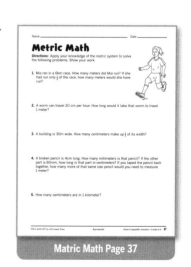

Matric Math Page 37

Metric Relay

Directions: Record your team's measurements in meters and centimeters below. Write down the total length that your collective balloons traveled.

Metric System		
Meter (m)	**Base**	
Centimeter (cm)	100 cm = 1m	
Millimeter (mm)	1000 mm = 1m	
	10 mm = 1cm	
Kilometer (km)	1000m = 1km	

Team Members

_____

_____

_____

_____

Score Card

METERS	CENTIMETERS

Metric Math

Directions: Apply your knowledge of the metric system to solve the following problems. Show your work.

1. Mia ran in a 6km race. How many meters did Mia run? If she had run only $\frac{1}{3}$ of the race, how many meters would she have run?

2. A worm can travel 20 cm per hour. How long would it take that worm to travel 1 meter?

3. A building is 30m wide. How many centimeters make up $\frac{1}{2}$ of its width?

4. A broken pencil is 4cm long. How many millimeters is that pencil? If the other part is 60mm, how long is that part in centimeters? If you taped the pencil back together, how many more of that same size pencil would you need to measure 1 meter?

5. How many centimeters are in 1 kilometer?

Situation Cell Phone

Standard
Data Analysis and Probability—Formulate questions that can be addressed with data and collect, organize, and display relevant data to answer them.

Objective
Students will select, create, and use appropriate graphical representations of data.

Anticipatory Set
Go to the front of the class with a worried look on your face. Tell students you received your cell phone bill and it is astronomical! Show ◄ students the **Cell Phone Bill (page 40)** on the overhead projector. Pretend you need students to help you figure out how to avoid going over your allotted minutes on your cell phone.

Purpose
Tell students they are going to collect data from cell phone bills, create a graph of the data, and analyze the data to determine the best solution to this dilemma.

Input
Lead a lesson on graphing. Remind students why graphs are useful and how they help people organize and analyze data. Show several types of graphs, including bar graphs, circle graphs, histograms, and line graphs. Discuss how different graphs represent different types of data and the importance of selecting the right graph for the data.

Modeling
Give copies of the Cell Phone Bill reproducible and the **Situation Cell Phone reproducible (page 41)** to students. Review the charges shown on the bill, and think aloud about why the overages are a problem. Ask students to determine how to represent the data. Guide the brainstorm around using a graph to show how many minutes you went over and how much that is costing. Encourage students to decide which type of graph would best

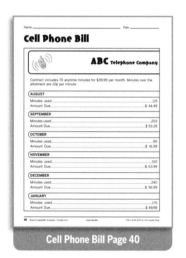

Cell Phone Bill Page 40

represent the data. Then tell students they can help you figure out which cell phone plan would best suit your calling habits.

Check for Understanding

Use a quick assessment technique to check for understanding. Ask students to put up their right hands if they understand what to do. Have them put up their left hands if they need more explanation. Provide more explanation as needed.

Guided Practice

Organize students into groups of two or three. Try to make sure each group has at least one student who has enough prior knowledge to perform the assigned task. Have them work together to graph the data on the cell phone bills. Remind students to focus on the minutes and cost each month which were over the allowed amount. Once the graph is complete, have students analyze the graph to determine patterns in the overage amounts. This information will help them evaluate three cell phone plans. Prompt students to make a recommendation for the best plan. Play background music with 60 beats per minute (no lyrics). Assist as needed.

Closure

Invite one person from each group to place a round dot sticker on the overhead transparency under the plan they feel would best meet the needs of the cell phone user. This will create a class graph of the results. Review this class graph. Invite volunteers to defend their positions if students disagree on the best plan. Have students answer the following questions in their math journals. *What was the hardest part of the assignment today? How do you think the skill you practiced today could help you in real life?*

The use of graphs provides a visual component to aid in retention.

Cell Phone Bill

ABC Telephone Company

Contract includes 70 anytime minutes for $39.99 per month. Minutes over the allotment are 10¢ per minute.

AUGUST

Minutes used...115
Amount Due...$ 44.49

SEPTEMBER

Minutes used...203
Amount Due...$ 53.29

OCTOBER

Minutes used..90
Amount Due...$ 41.99

NOVEMBER

Minutes used...310
Amount Due...$ 63.99

DECEMBER

Minutes used...240
Amount Due...$ 56.99

JANUARY

Minutes used...170
Amount Due...$ 49.99

Situation Cell Phone

Directions: Create a graph showing the data from the cell phone bill in the space below. Remember to label the graph.

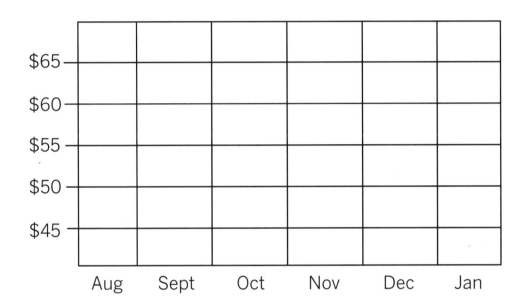

| | Aug | Sept | Oct | Nov | Dec | Jan |

$65 —
$60 —
$55 —
$50 —
$45 —

Directions: Circle the plan you think would best meet the needs of this cell phone user. Defend your answer in writing.

Plan A	**Plan B**	**Plan C**
Unlimited Minutes $69.99	100 minutes $29.99 +.15 per minute over	200 minutes $49.99 +.07 per minute over

_____

_____

_____

_____

Acting Out

Standard
Algebra—Use mathematical models to represent and understand quantitative relationships.

Objective
Students will solve word problems using body language and manipulatives.

Anticipatory Set
Make a transparency of **The Fox and the River reproducible (page 44)**, and read the problem aloud to students.

Purpose
Tell students they are going to use a method of problem solving called "acting out." They will use their bodies to solve a riddle.

Input
Instruct students about the usefulness of using people and objects to actually dramatize math problems as a tool for helping solve them. Movement stimulates blood flow to the brain, which can help the brain function better. Movement can also help check the feasibility of certain alternatives which may be difficult to visualize. Acting out may involve physically getting up and moving, or it may involve using objects to represent parts of the problem.

Modeling
After reading "The Fox and the River," show students how to act out the problem. Model how you want students to use their bodies to solve the problem. Ask three students to help you. Have them stand at the front of the room. Assign one person the role of hen, one person the role of corn, and the last person the role of fox. You will be the farmer. As the farmer, think aloud about different ways you can solve

the problem. Use the people in the group to help you act out the scene, thereby helping you find a solution. *Well, if I put the fox with the hen, the fox would eat the hen.* (Physically move the "fox" to the same side of the river as the "hen.") *So, I wouldn't want to do that. What if I put the fox on one side of the river and the hen on the other side of the river?* Continue in this manner until you figure out the solution. (The farmer takes the hen across the river and leaves it there. The farmer then returns for the fox and takes it across. The farmer takes the hen back across to the beginning side, leaves it there, and takes the corn. The farmer then returns for the hen.)

Check for Understanding

Use a quick assessment technique to check for understanding. Try the thumbs up for understanding and thumbs down for more explanation.

Guided Practice

Assign students to groups of four. Give each student a copy of **Acting Out Word Problems reproducible (page 45)**. Tell the class that each person in the group is going to represent a character in the word problem. Instruct them to work together to act out different scenarios to find a solution to the problem. Allow adequate time for groups to solve the problems. Remind them to record their answers on the reproducible and show their calculations if necessary. Roam around the room providing assistance as needed. Try to allow students some space to discover the solution, but guide them to avoid frustration.

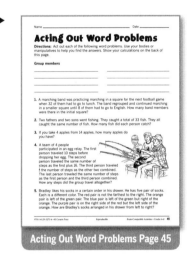

Acting Out Word Problems Page 45

Closure

Have each group act out one word problem for the class and share the answer.

Have students answer the following question in their math journals. *How can acting a problem out help you find a solution? Why do you think this is an effective strategy?*

The Fox and the River

A farmer stood near a river with a basket full of corn, a hen, and a fox. He looked despairingly at the boat which was supposed to carry him and his cargo across the river. It was too small to hold everything, and something would have to be left behind—but what? If he left the fox with the hen, the fox would eat the bird. If he left the hen with the corn, the hen would have a tasty meal. He could only take one item in the boat besides himself, but they all needed to cross the river. How can the farmer get himself and all of his cargo across the river safely?

Name _____ Date _____

Acting Out Word Problems

Directions: Act out each of the following word problems. Use your bodies or manipulatives to help you find the answers. Show your calculations on the back of this page.

Group members

_____   _____

_____   _____

_____   _____

_____   _____

1. A marching band was practicing marching in a square for the next football game when 32 of them had to go to lunch. The band regrouped and continued marching in a smaller square until 8 of them had to go to English. How many band members were there in the initial square?

2. Two fathers and two sons went fishing. They caught a total of 33 fish. They all caught the same number of fish. How many fish did each person catch?

3. If you take 4 apples from 14 apples, how many apples do you have?

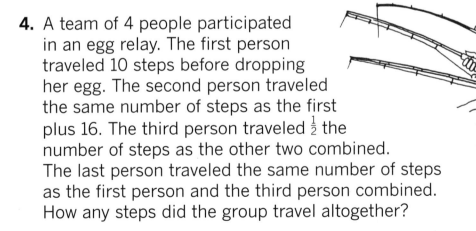

4. A team of 4 people participated in an egg relay. The first person traveled 10 steps before dropping her egg. The second person traveled the same number of steps as the first plus 16. The third person traveled $\frac{1}{2}$ the number of steps as the other two combined. The last person traveled the same number of steps as the first person and the third person combined. How any steps did the group travel altogether?

5. Bradley likes his socks in a certain order in his drawer. He has five pair of socks. Each is a different color. The red pair is not the farthest to the right. The orange pair is left of the green pair. The blue pair is left of the green but right of the orange. The purple pair is on the right side of the red but the left side of the orange. How are Bradley's socks arranged in his drawer from left to right?

CHAPTER 3

Social Studies

> Learning and retention are different. We can learn something for just a few minutes then lose it forever.

Social studies objectives lend themselves to brain-compatible teaching strategies. However, it is difficult for teachers to determine the main concepts on which to focus. Social studies texts, while a helpful resource, are filled with minute details which may not be vital to a child's understanding of the main ideas. If we want students to retain the information long-term, we have to be aware of how short- and long-term memory work. The brain of a young child can process only about five chunks of new information at a time. Therefore, if we want students to remember what we teach them, we have to limit the amount of material we cover and find ways to help them better retain what we do cover. The idea is to do a better job of teaching less.

Students can learn facts and information and hold the memory long enough to take a test. Retaining the information requires the learner to give conscious attention to facts and build conceptual frameworks to move the information into long-term memory. In social studies, students are often required to memorize important dates, names of people, and significant places. Rote rehearsal helps students remember facts for tests. Elaborative rehearsal, when students reprocess the information numerous times, requires students to discover relationships, make associations with prior learning, and interpret meaning. Elaborative rehearsal will help students remember those important dates, people, and places for much longer than next week's test.

Concept maps and visualization are a great way to help students make sense of new learning in social studies. Brain-compatible social studies instruction is as much fun for teachers as it is for students. Just remember, less is more!

1950s Hoop-la

Standard
Understand the ways human beings view themselves in and over time.

Objective
Students will compare pop culture in the United States in the 1950s with the present.

Anticipatory Set
Dress in clothing from the 1950s (poodle skirts, rolled up jeans, T-shirts, leather jackets), and play music from that time period. Try to use a hula-hoop as the music plays.

Purpose
Tell students they are going to research a few aspects of life in the United States during the 1950s and compare it to life in the United States today.

Input
Give students a brief background about the 1950s. Talk about the recovery from World War II and the technological advances the war brought to the United States. Spend some time showing pictures and talking about cultural icons from the period, such as cars, clothing, famous people, and toys or games. Frame the discussion around students' knowledge of life in the United States today. *How many of you have ever played with a hula-hoop? Did you know the hula-hoop was trademarked in the late 1950s by the Wham-O company and has sold millions worldwide?*

Modeling
Try to use the hula-hoop for its intended purpose. Keep it going for as long as you can. When it falls, make a joke about how you can find a better use for it. Tape the hula hoop on the board and label it *1950s*. Try again with another hula-hoop. When it falls, tape that hula-hoop to the board. Make sure it slightly overlaps with the other hoop. Label the second hula-hoop *Today*. Label the part that overlaps as *Both*. Use the hula-hoop diagram as a class Venn diagram and describe how to use it.

Make a photocopy of the **Toys and Games reproducible (page 50)** onto cardstock. Cut out the cards and distribute one to each student. Have students read the card and show a partner what the card says. If the

<table>
<tr><td colspan="3">Toys and Games</td></tr>
<tr><td>Hula-Hoops</td><td>Bicycles</td><td>Jacks</td></tr>
<tr><td>Video Games</td><td>Barbie®</td><td>Radio Shows</td></tr>
<tr><td>Frisbee®</td><td>Marbles</td><td>Rollerskates</td></tr>
<tr><td>Legos®</td><td>Dodgeball</td><td>Tiddlywinks</td></tr>
<tr><td>Building Blocks</td><td>Model Trains</td><td>Silly Putty®</td></tr>
<tr><td>Mr. Potato Head®</td><td>Hot Wheels®</td><td>Play Doh®</td></tr>
<tr><td>Cartoons</td><td>Toy Soldiers</td><td>Lincoln Logs™</td></tr>
<tr><td>Scrabble®</td><td>Transformers®</td><td>DVDs</td></tr>
<tr><td>Power Rangers®</td><td>Pogo Sticks</td><td>Slip 'N Slide®</td></tr>
<tr><td>Polly Pocket™</td><td>In-line Skates</td><td>View-Master®</td></tr>
<tr><td>Jenga®</td><td>UNO®</td><td>Checkers</td></tr>
<tr><td>Remote Control Cars</td><td colspan="2">Action Movie Figures</td></tr>
</table>

Toys and Games Page 50

students are unfamiliar with the toy or game on the card, ask them to discuss it with their partner. Describe the toys and games students don't know, or prompt students to do some research on the Internet.

Invite students to the board, and have them tape the card in the appropriate place on the hula-hoop diagram. Guide students as necessary. When all students have taped their cards to the board, read the diagram aloud.

Show students how they can use the information on the diagram to help them write a compare-and-contrast paragraph about the toys and games from the two time periods. The words in the center are the things the objects have in common. The two outside portions are the differences between the objects.

Check for Understanding

Ask students to participate in a "Hand Jive." Play lively 1950s music and show students how to do a hand jive. Add a special signal at the end of the hand movements to indicate understanding. For example, at the end of the song, students will show right hand on top if they understand and left hand on top if they do not understand. Review as necessary.

Guided Practice

Ask students to choose a topic they'd like to research. Encourage them to select a topic related to culture so they can compare the culture in the United States from today and the 1950s (music, television, social
◄ events, etc.). Give each student a copy of the **Research Notes reproducible (page 51)**. Allow students to use the Internet and library resources to gather information. Play background music with 60 beats per minute (no lyrics) during solo work. Circulate and assist as needed. Setting a timer helps with accountability and time management in multistep assignments.

Once students have finished the research, challenge them to organize the material on the **Venn Diagram (page 52)**. Then have them write a compare-and-contrast paragraph about culture in the 1950s and today. Direct them to use the **Paragraph reproducible (page 53)** and answer the reflection questions at the bottom of the page.

Research Notes Page 51

Closure

Invite students to read their paragraphs to the class. Have students respond to the following questions by sharing with a partner. *What are some of the most significant differences between life in the 1950s and today? What are some of the impacts of those changes?*

Independent Practice

Have students interview a friend or relative about his or her life during the 1950s. Prompt students to record what they learned in their journals. *Does the interviewee's recollection of life during that time period accurately reflect the information you found in your research? If not, what could explain the differences?*

"Using a tangible concept map helps learners make the transition from concrete to abstract."

Toys and Games

Hula-Hoops	Bicycles	Jacks
Video Games	Barbie®	Radio Shows
Frisbee®	Marbles	Rollerskates
Legos®	Dodgeball	Tiddlywinks
Building Blocks	Model Trains	Silly Putty®
Mr. Potato Head®	Hot Wheels®	Play Doh®
Cartoons	Toy Soldiers	Lincoln Logs™
Scrabble®	Transformers®	DVDs
Power Rangers®	Pogo Sticks	Slip 'N Slide®
Polly Pocket™	In-line Skates	View-Master®
Jenga®	UNO®	Checkers
Remote Control Cars		Action Movie Figures

Research Notes

Directons: Take notes on your topic in the space below.

My Topic: _____

Venn Diagram

Directions: Complete the diagram to show the similarities and differences between culture in the 1950s and today.

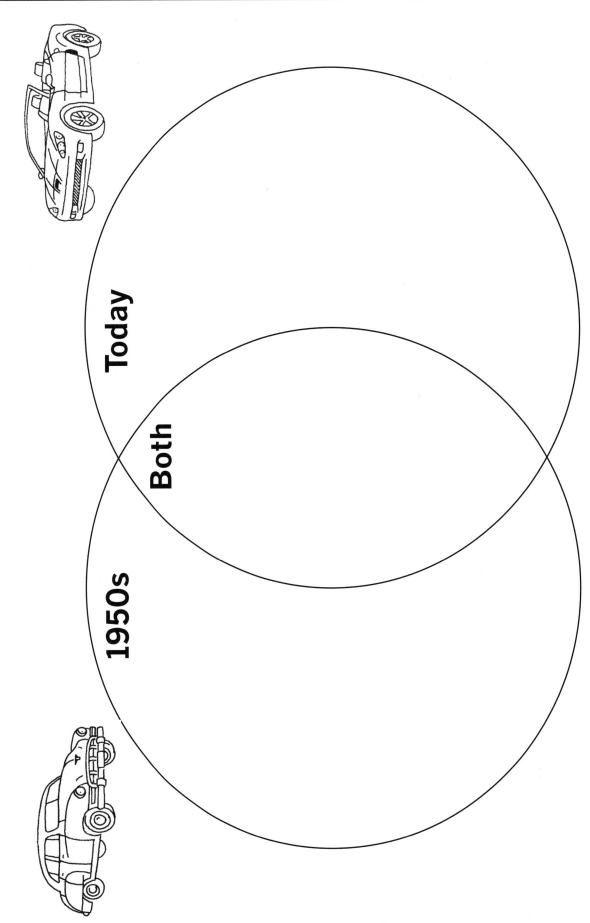

Today

Both

1950s

Paragraph

Directions: Write a compare-and-contrast paragraph.
Use the information from the Venn diagram.

_____
(topic)

_____

_____

_____

_____

_____

_____

_____

Directions: Answer the following reflection questions.

1. What are the main differences between life in the 1950s and life now that you discovered in your research?

_____

_____

_____

2. What impact do you think these differences have had on life today?

_____

_____

_____

Family Totem

Standard

Understand individual development and identity.

Objective

Students will create a family totem based on information learned about their ancestors.

Anticipatory Set

Select several objects that symbolize you and your interests or personality. For example, if you are the basketball coach, show a whistle and a basketball. Ask students to write down what the items symbolize about you. Invite students to share their responses with the class.

Purpose

Tell students they are going to research their family heritage and create symbols that reflect the people in their family.

Input

Talk to students about totem poles. Remind them of the origins of totem poles and how cultures use them to symbolize their heritage. Figures on the totems are usually animals, objects in nature, or people. The totem is a symbol of the history of a group of people.

Before students can create a family totem, they will have to learn about their family heritage. Be sensitive to students' home situations. Gladly accommodate any special needs as students are not able to learn if negative emotions are evoked.

PART 1

Modeling

◄ Give each student a copy of the **My Family reproducible (page 57)**. For the modeling portion of the lesson, make a transparency of the reproducible and demonstrate how to complete the task. Use your own family to show students where to write down the names of parents, grandparents, and great-grandparents. Point out where to prepare questions to ask relatives and the place to record the answers.

Give each student a copy of the **Family Tree reproducible (page 58)**. Demonstrate how to complete the family tree by recording the names of

My Family Page 57

parents, grandparents, and great-grandparents. In the interest of time, siblings and extended family have not been included. Tell students they will have two days to conduct the research and prepare the family tree.

Check for Understanding

Use a quick assessment technique to check for understanding. Ask students to show a smiling face if they understand or a frown if they do not understand. Explain again as necessary.

Guided Practice

Play background music with 60 beats per minute (no lyrics). Have students work individually to formulate questions to ask interviewees and list possible persons to interview. Students may fill in the family tree as they are able. This may help them ascertain the focus of their research. Circulate and assist students as they formulate their plans. Allow about fifteen minutes for students to prepare the questions.

Closure

Have students tell a partner who they plan to interview and some of the questions they plan to ask. Remind students they have two days to complete this part of the assignment.

Independent Practice

Students conduct interviews at home and complete the My Family reproducible.

PART 2

Modeling

Prior to the lesson, create a totem representing your family history. Use a unique symbol for each member of your family. Symbols can represent occupations, special features, or personality traits. Place the most distant ancestor at the bottom of the totem, and work up to yourself at the top. Include only yourself, your parents, grandparents, and great-grandparents.

Show your totem to the class. Discuss each symbol, and talk about the person it represents.

> **Background music can increase productivity.**

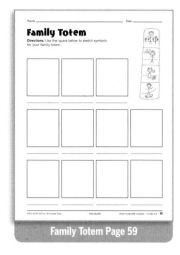

◀ Give each student a copy of the **Family Totem reproducible (page 59)**. Show students where they can sketch their ideas for the totem pole they will create. Indicate how you want students to create the totem and where to find the supplies.

Tell students to choose symbols that represent their family members and reflect something they learned about them during their research, such as nationality, personality traits, occupation, or another significant feature of their lives.

To create the totem pole, show students how to form a piece of posterboard into a roll (like a paper towel roll). Have them draw a final illustration of each symbol on a separate sheet of paper and color the symbols with bright colors. Tell students to glue the symbols onto the posterboard roll. Put the oldest ancestor's symbol at the bottom and each student's symbol at the top.

Check for Understanding

Ask a student to rephrase the instructions to check for understanding.

Guided Practice

Have students complete the plan and the totem. You may need to help students consider appropriate symbols for family members. Play background music (no lyrics) to promote creativity. Provide art supplies as needed.

Closure

Ask volunteers to share their totems with the class. Display all the totems in the classroom.

Have students reflect on the following questions in a journal. *What was one of the most significant thing you learned about your family as part of this assignment? How has your family heritage impacted who you are today?*

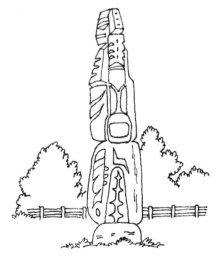

Name _____ Date _____

My Family

Directions: Use the lines provided to list names of possible family members or friends who could help you research information about your family heritage.

_____

_____

_____

_____

_____

_____

Directions: Use the lines below to write a few questions that will help you obtain the information you need about your family members. Consider questions about nationalities, occupations, personality traits, and things for which they are remembered.

Questions	Answers

Family Tree

Directions: Use the information you obtain to help you complete the family tree below. Include interesting facts about each person beside his or her name.

Great-grandparents

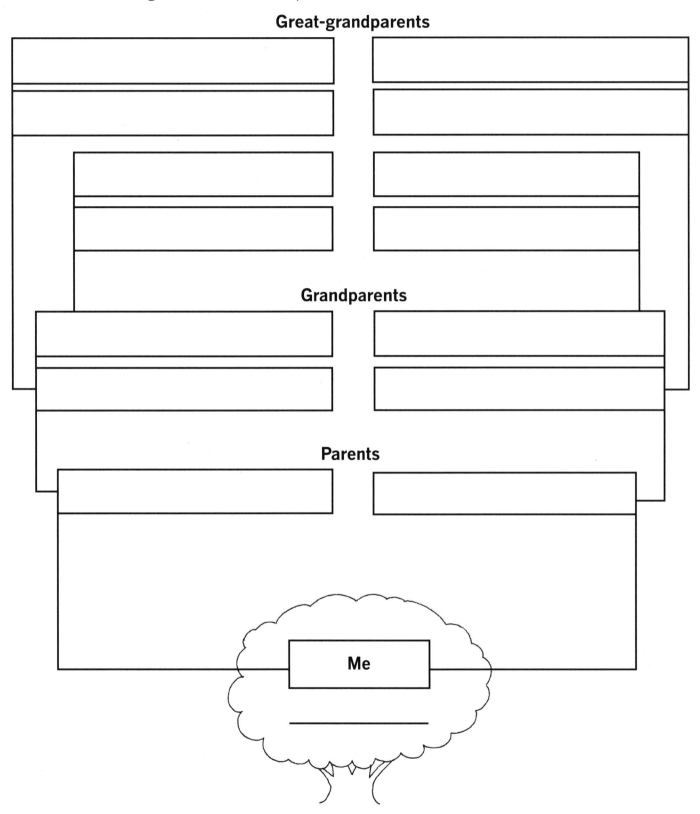

Grandparents

Parents

Me

Family Totem

Directions: Use the space below to sketch symbols for your family totem.

Guess Who?

Standard
Understand relationships among science, technology, and society.

Objective
Students will research and recall facts about famous historical figures.

Anticipatory Set
Begin with a game of "Guess Who?" Give students clues about a famous person in history. Start with the most obscure clue and end with the most recognizable clue. *Stand up when you think you know the person I am describing. The person is male. He is no longer alive. The person was a famous American. The person was instrumental in the American Revolution. The bust of this person is on the U.S. quarter. He was the first president of the United States.*

Purpose
This activity is designed to be used with a unit in the existing social studies textbook. The unit should contain some historical figures. Tell students they are going to play a guessing game to help them recall some of the facts about the historical figures they are studying.

Input
Help students focus by giving them some clues about what to pay attention to while reading. Point out the names of the figures you want them to pay attention to, and give a brief preview of who the person is. Have students read or skim the selection. Use a reading strategy appropriate for the learning level of the students.

Modeling

Guess Who? Page 62

◄ Give each student a copy of the **Guess Who reproducible (page 62)**. Model how to complete the task. Create an overhead transparency of the page, and show students how to find the information in the textbook and record it onto the reproducible. Then ask students to help you prepare the questions about the historical figure. Prompt them to figure out which detail is most obscure by asking them to name the least important thing to remember about this person. Then guide the discussion to help students create a question about the most obvious fact. *What is the most important thing to remember about this person?*

If appropriate, encourage students to use other resources to discover more about the historical figure.

Check for Understanding

Use a quick assessment technique to check for understanding.

Guided Practice

Assign a famous person for each student to research. If the unit contains a limited number of historical figures, assign students to work in groups. Ask students to complete the Guess Who? reproducible. Encourage them to use outside resources if information is limited in the textbook. Play background music (no lyrics) for solo work. Assist as needed.

When everyone has completed the reproducible, play the game you demonstrated at the beginning of the lesson. Have students stand up and find a partner. The first partner will read the facts in order from most obscure to most recognizable. The second partner must guess who the person is. Then the partners trade roles. Ask the students to find a new partner and repeat the process. Play the game as many times as students would like.

CLOSURE

Ask students to challenge you to a game of Guess Who? Allow students to ask you to guess the name of a historical figure based on clues they have written.

> **Novelty increases motivation and attention.**

Guess Who?

Name of historical figure: _____

Reason for fame: _____

_____

Interesting facts: _____

_____

_____

_____

Directions: Using the above information, create a list of facts about your person. Begin with the most obscure facts and end with the most recognizable.

1. _____

2. _____

3. _____

4. _____

5. _____

6. _____

7. _____

8. _____

9. _____

10. _____

To Vote or Not to Vote

Standard
Understand the ideals, principles, and practices of citizenship in a democratic republic.

Objective
Students will create a brochure to persuade eligible high school students to vote.

Anticipatory Set
Tell students that millions of Americans are eligible to vote and yet they do not exercise the right. Have students discuss with partners possible reasons why voter turnout for United States elections is so low.

Purpose
Tell students they are going to consider arguments for and against voting. They will create a brochure persuading eligible high school students to vote.

Input
On a piece of chart paper list the requirements for eligibility to vote. A voter must be 18 years old and a citizen of the United States. Ask students to think about why people don't exercise their right to vote. Allow adequate wait time. Encourage students to share their thoughts with a partner. Invite volunteers to share their discussion with the class, and record the responses on chart paper.

Now ask students to think about why people do exercise the right to vote. Allow adequate wait time. Have students share their thoughts with a partner. Invite volunteers to share their discussion with the class and, record the responses on chart paper.

Modeling
Students will be creating a persuasive brochure to convince high school students to vote. Prepare a sample prior to the lesson. Show the sample to the students, and explain the steps required to create the brochure. Write each step on the board as you describe it. Provide students with samples of other persuasive brochures.

Remind students that in a persuasive argument, the writer will understand the opponent's perspective and work hard to change that attitude. A good brochure uses quotations, pictures, and convincing arguments to persuade the reader. Make sure the students' work includes all of these elements.

Check for Understanding
Ask a student to explain the directions in his or her own words. Answer questions, or explain again as necessary.

Guided Practice
Divide students into groups of three or four students to complete the project. Provide references, art, and computer supplies as needed. Assist students with appropriate wording and concepts. Remind students that every member of the group must contribute something to the brochure. One student prepares the art, another conducts the research, and another student writes the text. Play background music with 60 beats per minute (no lyrics) to enhance creativity. Praise creative ideas and use of words.

Closure
Invite the groups to share their brochures with the class. Have students reflect on the learning by answering the following questions in their journals. *What did you learn about the importance of voting? What arguments would you give to someone who said they chose not to vote because their vote did not make a difference?*

Extension
Have your students contact the high schools in your area and distribute or display the brochures there. Take a field trip to the voting commissioner, and take copies of the brochures for her or him.

> "Real-life application of knowledge increases retention."

CHAPTER 4

Science

The scientific technology of the last two decades has made it possible for teachers to know more about how students learn than any of our predecessors. With this information comes excitement and challenge. It is up to us to use this new knowledge to foster a love of learning in the next generation. In the field of science, this is especially true.

For a brain to store information in long-term storage areas for future recall, the learning must make sense and have meaning. Brain scans have shown that when new learning is readily comprehensible (sense) and can be connected to the past experiences (meaning), there is substantially more cerebral activity followed by dramatically improved retention (Maquire, Frith, & Morris, 1999).

Making meaning has a tremendous impact on whether or not information will be stored. In order for students to retain the concepts they are learning, they must make a connection with their own experience. If that experience is a positive one, it is more likely the student will continue to actively participate in the learning. If the experience is negative, the student will likely turn off to the learning and store very little information.

Science curriculum can be viewed by students as relevant and filled with discovery, or it can be viewed as mundane memorization. The way in which we teach it makes the difference.

> **People will participate in learning activities that have yielded success for them and avoid those that have produced failure.**

We Will Rock You

Standard
Earth and Space Science—Understand structure of the earth system.

Objective
Students will research and teach the phases of the Rock Cycle to elementary students.

Anticipatory Set
Begin class by chanting the song *We Will Rock You*. Encourage students to stand up, clap and stomp, and chant along with you.

Purpose
Tell students they are going to learn about and research the rock cycle.

Input
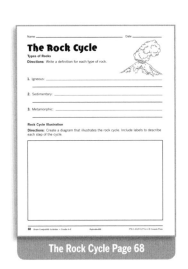

The Rock Cycle Page 68

Use the following activity during or after a unit on the rock cycle. Give each student a copy of **The Rock Cycle reproducible (page 68)**. Make a transparency of the reproducible, and show it on the overhead projector. As a class, define each type of rock and show examples if possible. Write the definitions on the transparency as students write on their papers. Discuss the rock cycle using the textbook or other resources.

Modeling
Tell students they are going to teach elementary students about the rock cycle. Before teachers teach, they must understand the topic and prepare a lesson. Students will have to determine the best way to teach the topic and then create the necessary materials for the "lesson." Offer the following suggestions: make a picture book, prepare a skit, or make a game. Whatever the groups choose to create, make sure the lesson contains accurate information and evidence of knowledge.

Check for Understanding
Use a quick assessment technique to check for understanding. Using the hand motions from "Rock, Paper, Scissors," ask students to show a rock if they understand or scissors if they do not understand.

Guided Practice

Divide the class into learning groups of up to four students. Assign groups based on the project students choose to complete. Remind them of what they already know about the rock cycle. Encourage them to learn more by doing research on the Internet and in books. Most Web sites about the rock cycle are educational in nature, but it is always good practice to monitor Internet use. On an individual basis, assist students who may have difficulty understanding the concept. Remind students to document URLs and take notes on the research. Background music with 60 beats per minute (no lyrics) can enhance productivity during group and solo work.

Give students ample opportunity to complete the project. If necessary, have students work on the project at home or over multiple class periods. However, enforce a deadline, and hold all students accountable for contributing to the project.

Closure

Have students "teach" a group of elementary students using their project. If elementary students are not nearby, videotape the lessons or teach other students in your school. Celebrate the lessons with rock candy and some rock-and-roll music.

Independent Practice

Encourage students to complete the **Rock Cycle Project Reflection reproducible (page 69)** at the end of the activity. Have students draw and label a diagram of the Rock Cycle as an assessment.

> **Allowing students to work independently or in groups provides an opportunity for differentiated instruction.**

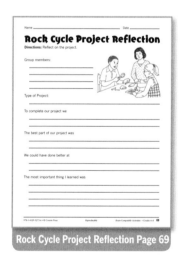

Rock Cycle Project Reflection Page 69

The Rock Cycle

Types of Rocks

Directions: Write a definition for each type of rock.

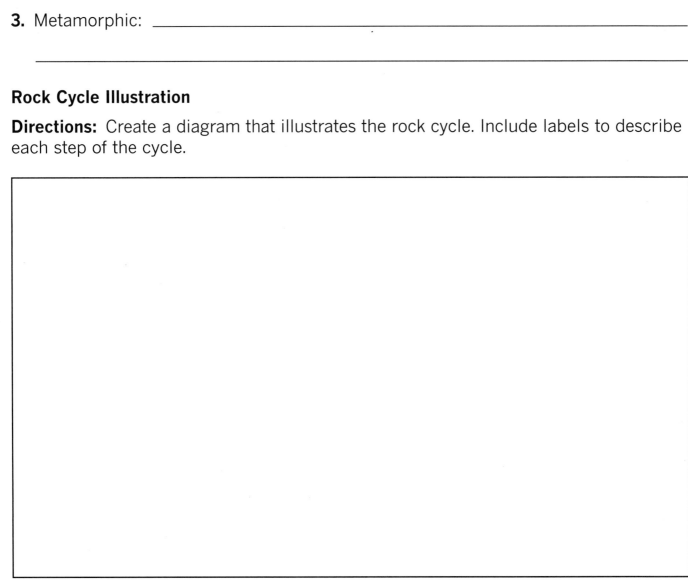

1. Igneous: _____

_____

2. Sedimentary: _____

_____

3. Metamorphic: _____

_____

Rock Cycle Illustration

Directions: Create a diagram that illustrates the rock cycle. Include labels to describe each step of the cycle.

Name ______________________ Date ____________

Rock Cycle Project Reflection

Directions: Reflect on the project.

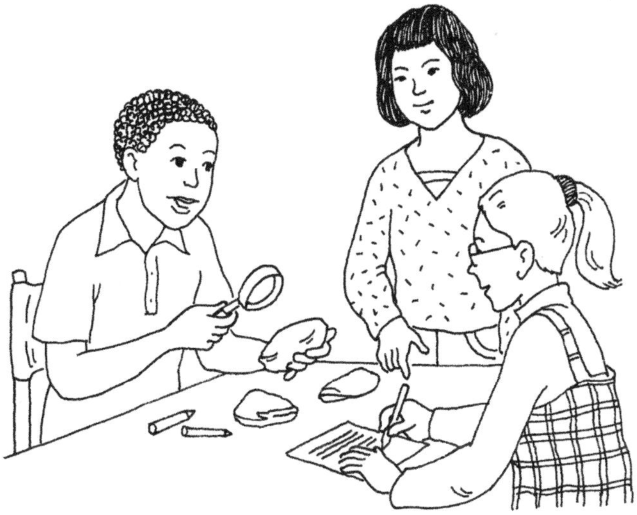

Group members:

____

____

____

____

Type of Project:

____

To complete our project we

____

____

The best part of our project was

____

____

We could have done better at

____

____

The most important thing I learned was

____

____

____

____

Mitosis Focus

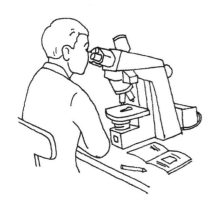

Standard
Life Science—Understand structure and function in living systems.

Objective
Students will create a mnemonic device to aid in the recall of the phases of mitosis.

Anticipatory Set
Ask all students to stand up. Assign one student as the parent cell. The parent cell must tag other students to assemble enough "material" for cell division. When a student is tagged by the parent cell, he or she attaches to become part of the parent cell. When the parent cell consists of six people, it experiences mitosis and splits into two cells, each with three people. Each of these cells then become parent cells and continues the game until all students are part of a group of three. Have students sit down with their new team of three. Tag games have tremendous focusing power because they evoke a safe amount of "fight or flight" hormones. Teachers must be creative, however, regarding safety in the classroom. Set rules concerning the speed of play, the type of interpersonal interaction, and the care of the classroom.

Purpose
Tell students they are going to learn about mitosis today and create a mnemonic device to help them remember.

Input
◄ Give each student a copy of **Phases of Mitosis (page 72)** reproducible. Read the phases loud, and ask students to repeat the correct pronunciation. Give a brief lesson about each phase, and try to incorporate multisensory approaches into the learning. Many Web sites offer great interactive mitosis tutorials.

Modeling
Write some common mnemonics on the board or overhead. For example, *Please Excuse My Dear Aunt Sally* (operations in math) or *Never Eat Slimy Worms* (directions on a compass rose).

Tell students that developing a mnemonic can help them to remember something. In this case, students are going to create a

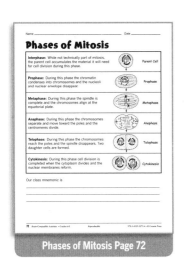

Phases of Mitosis Page 72

mnemonic about the phases of mitosis using the first letter of each phase. Instruct students to use words that have meaning for them.

Check for Understanding

Ask the groups to discuss the instructions. When everyone in the group understands what to do, have the group raise their hands.

Guided Practice

Have students work with their groups to develop a mnemonic device for the stages of mitosis. Play background music with 60 beats per minute (no lyrics). Circulate among the teams and assist as needed. Give students about 15 minutes for this assignment.

Closure

Call on random team members to share their mnemonics. Have students vote by secret ballot for their choice for the class mnemonic. Reassure students that they may continue to use their own mnemonic device for individual study if it helps them. A class choice is simply needed for ease of instruction and review. Have students write the class mnemonic on the bottom of the Phases of Mitosis Reproducible.

Independent Practice

Have students complete the **Mitosis Cartoon Reproducible (page 73)** for homework. This assignment encourages students to draw pictures to help them recall the phases of mitosis and the class mnemonic.

> **Mnemonics aids in retention by establishing meaning.**

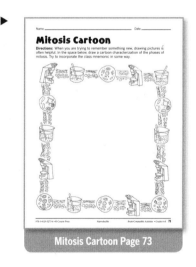

Mitosis Cartoon Page 73

Phases of Mitosis

Interphase: While not technically part of mitosis, the parent cell accumulates the material it will need for cell division during this phase.		Parent Cell
Prophase: During this phase, the chromatin condenses into chromosomes, and the nucleoli and nuclear envelope disappear.	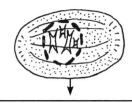	Prophase
Metaphase: During this phase, the spindle is complete, and the chromosomes align at the equatorial plate.	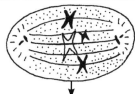	Metaphase
Anaphase: During this phase, the chromosomes separate and move toward the poles, and the centromeres divide.	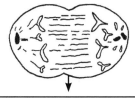	Anaphase
Telophase: During this phase, the chromosomes reach the poles, and the spindle disappears. Two daughter cells are formed.	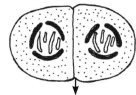	Telophase
Cytokinesis: During this phase, cell division is completed when the cytoplasm divides and the nuclear membranes reform.		Cytokinesis

Our class mnemonic is

_____

_____

_____

Mitosis Cartoon

Directions: When you are trying to remember something new, drawing pictures is often helpful. In the space below, draw a cartoon characterization of the phases of mitosis. Try to incorporate the class mnemonic in some way.

Heart Walk

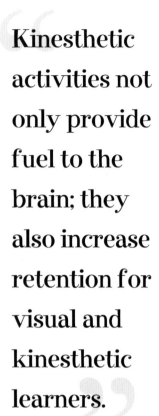

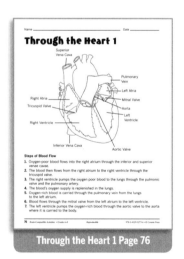

Through the Heart 1 Page 76

Standard
Life Science—Understand structure and function in living systems.

Objective
Using a kinesthetic model, students will recall the path of blood flow through the heart.

Anticipatory Set
Have students stand, do 20 jumping jacks, and then sit back down. Show students how to take their pulse in their wrists. Explain that the pulse is the blood flowing through one's body.

Purpose
Tell students they are going to learn the path blood takes as it flows through the heart.

Input
Make a transparency of the **Blood Flow Through the Heart 1 reproducible (page 76)**. Give each student his or her own copy. Review the path of blood flow through the heart, and have students use their fingers to trace the path on their own papers. Point to each part of the heart as ◄ you talk about it. If students have difficulty with pronunciation, ask them to repeat the words after you say them.

Modeling
Prior to the lesson, set up a giant outline of a heart. You can use chalk on the playground, tape on the floor of the gym, or orange cones on the field. The outline of the heart must be large enough for students to walk through. Create the path that blood travels through the heart. Label the important parts of the heart as seen on the Blood Flows Through the Heart reproducible.

During the lesson, take students to the giant "heart." Ask them to form a single-file line and follow you through the heart. As you walk through the heart, describe the anatomical features of the heart. When you are in the oxygen-poor places, put a frown on your face. When you are in the oxygen-rich places, put a smile on your face. (As an alternative, use happy- and sad-face paper masks.)

Check for Understanding

Tell students they are going to walk the path of blood flow through the heart just as they did as a class. Check for understanding by asking a student to explain the instructions.

Guided Practice

Have the students walk in small groups through the parts of the heart following the path that blood flows. Students should use smiles and frowns to indicate whether the blood is oxygen-rich or oxygen-poor as it goes through different regions of the heart. Students should identify the parts of the heart as they go through each one. Students who are not currently walking through the heart should practice tracing the blood flow with their fingers on the worksheets. After students have done this as a group with your assistance, challenge them to walk in pairs or individually.

Closure

Give students a copy of **Blood Flow Through the Heart 2 reproducible (page 77)**. The reproducible contains the same diagram as the first reproducible except it is missing labels and words. Give students two minutes to fill in as many of the labels as possible and draw arrows indicating the direction of blood flow. After two minutes, have students play "Find Someone Who…" to complete the rest of the reproducible. Students will mingle around the room, find a partner with whom to exchange one answer, and then find another partner to repeat the process. Allow five minutes to complete the worksheet in this manner.

▶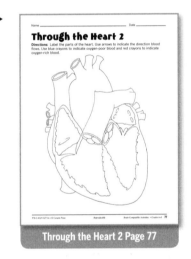

Through the Heart 2 Page 77

Independent Practice

Allow students to independently walk through the heart identifying parts and blood flow. This also serves as a great kinesthetic assessment tool.

Through the Heart 1

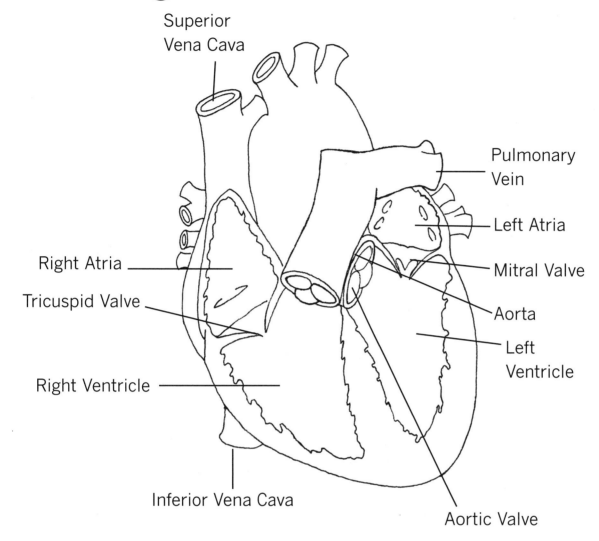

Superior
Vena Cava

Pulmonary
Vein

Left Atria

Mitral Valve

Right Atria

Tricuspid Valve

Aorta

Left
Ventricle

Right Ventricle

Inferior Vena Cava

Aortic Valve

Steps of Blood Flow

1. Oxygen-poor blood flows into the right atrium through the inferior and superior venae cavae.
2. The blood then flows from the right atrium to the right ventricle through the tricuspid valve.
3. The right ventricle pumps the oxygen-poor blood to the lungs through the pulmonic valve and the pulmonary artery.
4. The blood's oxygen supply is replenished in the lungs.
5. Oxygen-rich blood is carried through the pulmonary vein from the lungs to the left atrium.
6. Blood flows through the mitral valve from the left atrium to the left ventricle.
7. The left ventricle pumps the oxygen-rich blood through the aortic valve to the aorta, where it is carried to the body.

Through the Heart 2

Directions: Label the parts of the heart. Use arrows to indicate the direction blood flows. Use blue crayons to indicate oxygen-poor blood and red crayons to indicate oxygen-rich blood.

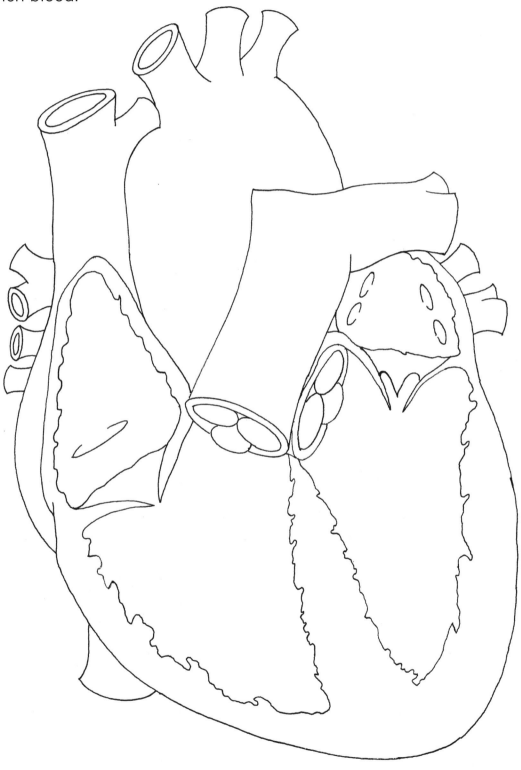

Picturing Chemical Equations

Standard

Physical Science—Understand properties and changes of properties in matter.

Objective

Students will be able to show the principle of balanced chemical equations with the use of pictures.

Anticipatory Set

Show students a set of scales that have more weight on one end than the other. Ask students to think about what you would have to do to balance the scales. Guide the discussion so students see that you have to take weight away from one side or add weight to one side.

Purpose

Tell students they are going to begin to learn how to balance chemical equations.

Input

The Conservation Law of Matter says that the total mass of reactants must equal the total mass of the product. In other words, the same number of each kind of atom must be on both sides of the equation—similar to the balanced scale. Write $Fe + S \rightarrow FeS$ on the board. Tell students: *The equation $Fe + S \rightarrow FeS$ is a balanced equation for sulfur because there is the same number of each type of atom on each side* (1). Write $H_2 + Cl_2 \rightarrow HCl$ on the board. Explain: *The equation $H_2 + Cl_2 \rightarrow HCl$ is not a balanced equation for hydrochloric acid, however. There are 2 H and 2 Cl on the left, but only 1 of each on the right.*

Refer back to the earlier experiment with the scales in which you determined that the way to balance weight was to either add weight to one side or take it away from the other. Explain that for chemical equations, no atoms can be destroyed; therefore, one can't take away an atom from one side. The only option is to add atoms until the sides are equal. Often this can be done by adding a single atom to one side. Other times, it gets a little more complicated because increasing the atoms on one side impacts the other. In those cases, just keep playing with the numbers until you find a solution that works. (Note: Do not include the higher levels of learning unless students are ready.)

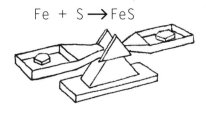

$Fe + S \rightarrow FeS$

In the example above, if we increase the HCl to 2, we get a balanced equation. It would look like this: $H_2 + Cl_2 \rightarrow 2HCl$. These concepts are very abstract, however, and using pictures to represent the atoms in the equations will help students better understand.

Modeling

Make multiple photocopies of the **Apples and Trees reproducible (page 80)**. Cut out the shapes and tape the apples and trees on the board so everyone can see. Tell students the apples and trees will represent the atoms in the equation. Place 2 apples and 2 trees on the left side of the equation and place 1 apple and 1 tree on the right side. Write the equation above the pictures. Point out that the pictures make it easy to see the equation is not equal. Challenge students to tell you how to make the equation equal. *We need to add another apple in a tree to this side. I can do that by putting a 2 in front of the whole product on the right. Then I can add another apple in a tree to the right side of the equation, making both sides balance.*

Check for Understanding

Use a quick assessment technique to check for understanding.

Guided Practice

Give students a copy of the **Picturing Chemical Equations reproducible (page 81)**. Instruct them to first draw pictures to represent the atoms in the equation. Then have students determine how many atoms are needed to balance the pictures on both sides and draw those pictures. Allow students to get help from partners or team members. Circulate and provide individual instruction as needed.

Closure

Write the answers to the equations on the board. Have students share their work with their learning group. Invite volunteers to share with the class.

> The use of pictures or manipulatives helps make abstract concepts more concrete.

▶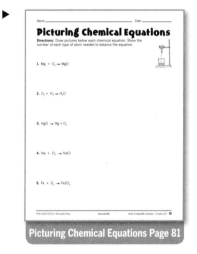

Picturing Chemical Equations Page 81

Apples and Trees

Picturing Chemical Equations

Directions: Draw pictures below each chemical equation. Show the number of each type of atom needed to balance the equation.

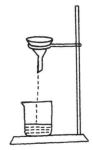

1. $Mg + O_2 \rightarrow MgO$

2. $O_2 + H_2 \rightarrow H_2O$

3. $HgO \rightarrow Hg + O_2$

4. $Na + Cl_2 \rightarrow NaCl$

5. $Fe + O_2 \rightarrow Fe2O_3$

CHAPTER 5

Physical Education and the Arts

> We have never discovered a culture on this planet—past or present—that doesn't have music, art and dance.

Observe any preschool classroom, and you will see students singing, dancing, and drawing. These activities enhance learning for young children. Cognitive areas of the brain are developing as children finger-paint, sing songs, chant rhymes, and dance. The cognitive benefits of these activities continue throughout childhood and into young adulthood, yet art and music classes are the first to be eliminated during school budget cuts. Art, music, and movement should be prominentaly featured in any middle school classroom.

Music

Listening to music provides therapeutic benefits; however, there are educational benefits as well. Research studies have shown a strong correlation between music and achievement in mathematics. Music and math share several concepts: patterns, geometry, counting, ratios, proportions, equivalent fractions, and sequences. Therefore, developing the cognitive areas of the brain with music can enhance the skills needed for mathematical tasks.

Visual Arts

Imagery is visualization in the mind's eye of something a person has actually experienced. The more information an image contains, the richer and more vibrant it becomes. Students can be taught to use imagery to enhance learning and increase retention. Teachers should integrate imagery as a regular classroom strategy across the curriculum.

Movement

The more scientists study the cerebellum, the more we realize that movement and learning are inescapably linked. Physical movement increases blood flow and brings oxygen to the brain. Higher levels of oxygen in the blood significantly enhance cognitive performance. Dance, specifically, helps students become more aware of their physical presence, spatial relationships, breathing, timing, and rhythm. Engaging other cerebral aptitudes enhances integration of sensory perception.

Personal Petroglyphs

Objective

Students will create images similar to ancient petroglyphs to represent themselves.

Anticipatory Set

On the board, draw the following pictures in a line: an eye, a heart, an apple, and several stick figures. Give each student a sticky note. Ask them to write down what they think the petroglyph means. Allow two minutes for students to write. Prompt students to place their sticky notes on the board next to the message. Read some of the notes aloud.

Purpose

Tell students they are going to create a petroglyph that will communicate something about themselves.

Input

Before written words were developed, ancient people used petroglyphs to communicate. Petroglyphs are actually images carved into stone. They are different from pictographs or hieroglyphics, which were painted. Petroglyphs have been discovered in most areas of the world, and many date back to Neolithic times. No one is certain exactly what the petroglyphs mean or how they were used.

Use the Internet or print resources to show students several examples of petroglyphs. Talk about how the ancient cultures used symbols for communication much as we use words today.

Petroglyph Prep Page 85

Modeling

Make a copy of the **Petroglyph Prep reproducible (page 85)** for each student. Place a transparency of the same reproducible on an overhead projector. Demonstrate how to complete the reproducible by using yourself as an example. Think aloud as you answer the prompts. When you are considering an image that would represent you, consider the things you like or characteristics about your personality that may be similar to an animal. Are you as clever as a fox? Are you someone who is a keen observer like an eagle, or are your most beautiful aspects on the inside, like a pearl in an oyster? First decide what animal or object would best represent you, and then create a simple image of it.

When you refer back to the petroglyph examples you showed in the Input part of the lesson, point out how simple the drawings are. They clearly articulate a message, but the drawings are simple line drawings. This is important because the petroglyphs were carved into stone.

Check for Understanding

Ask a students to explain the instructions as a check for understanding.

Guided Practice

Give each student a copy of the Petroglyph Prep reproducible. Direct them to complete the worksheet carefully as a guide to help decide what image to create. Encourage students to practice the petroglyph on paper before carving it into clay.

Provide necessary art supplies for students, including clay and carving tools. Instruct students to create the petroglyph on the clay tablet. Play background music with 60 beats per minute (no lyrics) to stimulate creativity. Provide encouragement to students who find creative assignments difficult.

Closure

Display all the petroglyphs, and invite students to talk about their work. Can you guess whose is whose by analyzing the symbols?

Independent Practice

Have students research petroglyphs on the Internet and answer the following questions. *How are the petroglyphs from different parts of the world different from one another? How are they similar? How would you explain the fact that similar petroglyph images have been found in remote parts of the world?*

Petroglyph Prep

Directions: Answer the following questions and prompts. Then carve a petroglyph into a clay tablet.

Brainstorm characteristics or traits about yourself in the space below.

_____

_____

_____

_____

_____

Look at your list of traits. Are they similar to any animals or objects in nature? List those below.

_____

_____

Circle the animal or object you feel best describes you. Consider simple ways to draw that animal or object. Sketch your ideas below.

```



```

Mozart Metaphors

Objective
Students will write and illustrate metaphors inspired by Mozart's music.

Anticipatory Set
Play Mozart classics as students enter the classroom. Write an example of a simile and a metaphor on the board. *The clouds are like soft feathers on a dove* (simile). *The pain was a knife to my heart* (metaphor). Allow students to get settled, and then ask them to tell you the difference between a simile and a metaphor. Give a topic, and tell students to create as many metaphors as they can about that topic. Encourage students to share their ideas with a partner before sharing with the entire class.

If students do not demonstrate a clear understanding of the difference between similes and metaphors, provide direct instruction before proceeding with the activity.

Purpose
Tell students they are going to listen to music and create a metaphor for the music.

Input
Give a little background information about Mozart. Talk about how music can increase creativity and other brain functions. Discuss how listening to music affects people in different ways. Encourage students to think critically about the gifts of the music and avoid making a judgment about the type of music.

Modeling
Model what you want students to do. Start by demonstrating how to quietly listen to the music. Close your eyes if you can. Listen attentively, and keep your mind open and free of distractions. Just listen and concentrate on how the music makes you feel. What comes to mind while you are listening? Think aloud as you demonstrate the task.

◄ Show students a transparency of the **Mozart Metaphors reproducible (page 88)**. Demonstrate how they should complete the worksheet. Use your own ideas about the current piece of music to answer the prompts. When you choose your favorite metaphor, show students what materials you will use to make a visual image of it. Write the metaphor on the illustration.

Mozart Metaphors Page 88

Check for Understanding

Use a quick assessment technique to check for understanding. Try having students write *yes* or *no* on a piece of scrap paper. If they understand what to do, ask them to hold up the word *yes*. If they do not understand, ask them to hold up the word *no*. Review the instructions as necessary.

Guided Practice

Play a different piece of music by Mozart. Give students a copy of the Mozart Metaphor reproducible as they are listening. Hold students accountable for remaining silent as they listen and brainstorm metaphor ideas. Assist students with the wording of the metaphor. Provide art supplies for the illustrations, and require students' best work. Continue to play Mozart as background music while students work.

Closure

Have students share their metaphors and illustrations. Display them in the classroom.

Independent Practice

Have students research and prepare a report on the life and work of Mozart.

Name _____ Date _____

Mozart Metaphors

Directions: Respond to each prompt. On a separate piece of paper, illustrate the metaphor. Write the metaphor on your illustration.

1. Listen to the piece of music. List ideas or images that come to mind as you listen.

_____

_____

_____

_____

_____

2. Refer to your list of ideas. Circle the one you like the best. Use the lines below to practice different versions of your metaphor.

_____

_____

_____

_____

3. Circle the metaphor you think best represents the music. Sketch an illustration for that metaphor below as a rough draft before you begin your work on art paper.

Cartoons Can Teach

Objective

Students will create cartoons to enhance memory retention of text book chapters and vocabulary words.

Anticipatory Set

Read an age-appropriate cartoon to students. Try the newspaper, children's magazines, or comic books. Enjoy the laugh!

Purpose

Tell students they are going to create a cartoon to help them remember content they are currently studying.

Input

Many subjects in school require students to memorize information. Regardless of the content, the use of cartoons has been found to make learning more fun and more memorable. Talk to students about the benefit of humor and visual images in retaining information. Tell them: *The hormones produced in your brain when you feel good can actually help you retain some of the information you have learned. Drawing pictures that relate to the learning can aid in retention.* Cartoons meet both of those categories.

Modeling

Make an overhead transparency of the **Cartoons Can Teach reproducible (page 91)**. Demonstrate how to complete the task. On the first example, use a vocabulary word most students would know. Think aloud as you say the word, recite the definition, and create a cartoon for the word. *When you want to create a cartoon to help you recall a vocabulary word, the first thing you need to do is associate the word with something you already know. Does the vocabulary word sound like another word? Does the meaning conjure up a scene in your mind? For example, the word 'embark' sounds like the word 'bark'. I can remember the word embark means 'to set out on a journey' by picturing a canoe made out of bark. I can draw a great picture that would help me remember that. If I made my picture humorous, it would even be that much easier to recall.*

On the second example, use the flow map to show how to recall events in a textbook chapter. Think aloud as you draw pictures of all the main parts of the text. Because you can only include so much in a comic strip, select the most important facts to include.

> ## Humor increases novelty and motivation.

Cartoons Can Teach Page 91

Check for Understanding

Ask students to turn to a partner and restate the instructions for the activity. Invite a volunteer to give the class instructions once more. Explain again as needed.

Guided Practice

Give each student a copy of the Cartoons Can Teach reproducible. Direct them to complete the worksheet for either a vocabulary word they are studying or a chapter in a textbook. As an alternative, coordinate with a content area teacher, and give the students a word or chapter to work with. Play background music to enhance productivity during solo work. Circulate and assist as needed. Provide art supplies.

Closure

Invite students to share and display their cartoons. Create a special bulletin board, or post the cartoons in the content area classroom as a study guide.

Cartoons Can Teach

Directions: Draw a cartoon for a single topic here.

Directions: Draw cartoons for a series of events here.

Fitness Instructor

Objective
Students will work as a group to design a fitness program.

Anticipatory Set
On a piece of chart paper, write the words *Get Fit.* Ask students to think for one minute about all of the exercises people can do to get fit. Encourage students to write their ideas on a piece of scrap paper to help them remember. Have students share their lists with a partner. Invite volunteers to share their ideas with the class. Record the exercises on the chart paper.

Purpose
Tell students they are going to work with a group to create a fitness program and demonstrate it for the class.

Input
Review the benefits of exercise and different types of exercises. Ask students: *Why do people need exercise? What is the difference between aerobic and anaerobic exercise? Why are both important?* Ask students to think about what exercises they do at home, at school, or in organized groups. Talk about how and why people organize their exercises into fitness programs.

Modeling

Show students an example of a fitness program. You can find many examples at a local health club or fitness center. Challenge students to identify the goal of the program and each of the exercises listed. If possible, demonstrate any exercises students do not know, or invite a guest speaker to class.

Give each student a copy of the **Fitness Program reproducible (page 94)**. Explain and model how to complete the task. Start by determining the goal for the program and the exercises that will help attain the goal. Then offer recommendations for the user, and suggest appropriate music to accompany the program. Finally, demonstrate the fitness program you designed.

Check for Understanding

Use a quick assessment technique to check for understanding. Ask students to show one finger for understanding and two fingers if they need more explanation.

Fitness Program Page 94

Guided Practice

Ask students to form groups of three or four. Tell them they are going to create a fitness program for other middle school students. Completing the reproducible will help to organize their thoughts. Encourage members of the group to talk about and try out the exercises before including them in the program to make sure they meet the goal.

Allow students access to the Internet and fitness resources to help them make decisions. Encourage students to find appropriate music to accompany the program. (Note: Remind students that music must be approved for all audiences.)

Closure

Have students demonstrate the fitness program they created and explain each exercise as they demonstrate. Prompt the other students to ask questions.

Independent Practice

Have students reflect on the activity in their journals. Ask them to respond to the following questions. *What was the most valuable thing I learned from this activity? How can I incorporate fitness into my life? Why is fitness important to me?*

Name ______________________________ Date ______________

Fitness Program

Directions: Create a fitness program for a middle-school students.

Fitness Goal ______________________________

Exercises

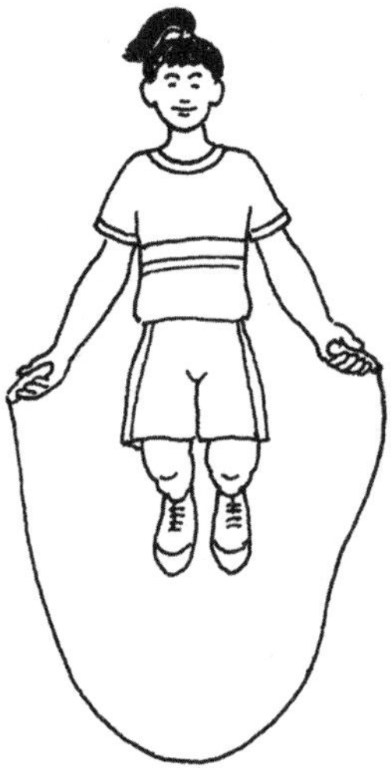

Recommendations

Music

Answer Key

HINK PINK THINK! (PAGE 27)
1. fat cat
2. big pig
3. black sack
4. hyper diaper
5. last blast
6. cold gold
7. ants pants
8. teeny bikini
9. bare chair
10. gritty kitty or shabby tabby
11. boat vote
12. far car

IS IT A DEAL? (PAGE 33)
Jeans:	$24
	$19
	$65
	$23.20
Shoes:	N/A
	$50 or $75
	$59.99
	$32
Shirts:	$11.99
	$12
	$12 or $24 (3)
	$12.80
Backpack:	$24 or $15
	N/A
	$21
	$24 or $16

METRIC MATH (PAGE 37)
1. 6000, 2000
2. 5 hours
3. 1500cm
4. 40mm; 6cm; 9 more
5. 100,000cm

ACTING OUT WORD PROBLEMS (PAGE 45)
1. 81 band members
2. 11 fish (father, son, and grandfather)
3. You have 4 apples
4. 82 steps
5. Red, Purple, Orange, Blue, Green

PICTURING CHEMICAL EQUATIONS (PAGE 81)
1. $2Mg + 1 O_2 \rightarrow 2 MgO$
2. $1 O_2 + 2 H_2 \rightarrow 2 H_2O$
3. $2 HgO \rightarrow 2 Hg + 1 O_2$
4. $2 Na + Cl_2 \rightarrow 2 NaCl$
5. $6 Fe + 3 O_2 \rightarrow 3 Fe2O_3$

References

Armstrong, L. (n.d.). *Interactive Rock Cycle Animation*. Retrieved August 12, 2006, from www.classzone.com/books/earth_science/terc/content/investigations/es0602/es0602page02.cfm?chapter_no=investigation.

Burchers, S. (1998). *Vocabulary cartoons*. Punta Gorda, FL: New Monic Books.

Draze, D. (2003). *Red hot root words*. San Luis Obispo, CA: Dandy Lion Publications.

Dun, S. (2005). Classic chembalancer. *Funbased learning: Chemistry*. Retrieved August 11, 2006, from http://funbasedlearning.com/chemistry/chembalancer/default.htm.

Gatten, B. (n.d.). *Sparknote on Alice in Wonderland and through the looking glass*. Retrieved August 11, 2006, from http://sparknotes.com/lit/alice/.

Gurian, M., & Henley, P. (2001). *Boys and girls learn differently!* San Francisco, CA: Jossey-Bass.

Heart monitor unit. (n.d.). Retrieved August 11, 2006, from http://www.shodor.org/ssep/prl/duketech/techtronics/lessons/heart_monitor/heart_background.htm.

Helmenstine, A. M. (2007). *Balancing chemical equations*. Retrieved August 11, 2006, from http://chemistry.about.com/cs/stoichiometry/a/aa042903a.htm.

How does blood flow through the heart? (2002). Retrieved August 11, 2006, from www.clevelandclinic.org/heartcenter/pub/guide/heartworks/bloodflow.htm.

Idiom [Electronic version]. *Merriam Webster Dictionary*. (2007). Retrieved August 4, 2006, from http://www.m-w.com/dictionary/idiom.

Kagan, S. (1994). *Cooperative learning*. San Clemente, CA: Kagan Publishing.

Kagan, S. (2000). *Silly sports and goofy games*. San Clemente, CA: Kagan Publishing.

Maquire, E. A., Frith, C. D., & Morris, R. G. M. (1999). The functional neuroanatomy of comprehension and memory: The importance of prior knowledge. *Brain, 122*, 1839-1850.

Mitosis: Labeled diagram. (1999). Retrieved August 12, 2006, from the National Health Museum's Access Excellence Web site: http://www.accessexcellence.org/RC/VL/GG/mitosis.html.

Moncur, M. (1994). Quotations by subject: democracy. *The quotations page*. Mercur, Michael. Retrieved August 12, 2006, from http://www.quotationspage.com/subjects/democracy/.

Music and color. *A lifetime of color: Create art*. (1998). Retrieved August 4, 2006, from http://www.sanford-artedventures.com/create/try_this_music.html

Nordgaarden, C. (1995). *Create a culture*. Santa Barbara, CA: The Learning Works, Inc.

Quinion, M. (n.d.). Raining cats and dogs. *Worldwide words*. Retrieved March 22, 2007, from http://www.worldwidewords.org/qa/qa-rai1.htm.

The rock cycle. (2001). Retrieved August 12, 2006 from http://www.minsocam.org/MSA/K12/rkcycle/rkcycleindex.html.

The rock cycle. (2005). Retrieved August 12, 2006 from Wheeling Jesuit University's Center for Education Technology Web site: http://www.cet.edu/ete/modules/msese/earthsysflr/rock.html.

Sousa, D. A. (2006). *How the brain learns, 3rd Edition*. Thousand Oaks, CA: Corwin Press.

Sullivan, J. (2006). The cell cycle. *Cells alive: Cell biology*. Retrieved August 12, 2006 from http://www.cellsalive.com/cell_cycle.htm.